Carefree ENTERTAINING

MABLE & GAR
HOFFMAN

FISHER
BOOKS

Publishers: Bill Fisher
                  Helen Fisher
                  Howard Fisher

Editors: Joyce Bush
                  Helen Fisher

Art Director: Josh Young
Drawings: David Fischer
Photos: DeGennaro Associates
Book Production: Paula Peterson
                  Nancy Taylor

Published by Fisher Books
PO Box 38040
Tucson, AZ 85740-8040
(602) 292-9080

Copyright 1991 Fisher Books

Printed in U.S.A.
Printing 10 9 8 7 6 5 4 3 2

**Library of Congress
Cataloging-in-Publication Data**

Hoffman, Mable
    Carefree entertaining / Mable & Gar
Hoffman.
        p.   cm.
    Includes index.
    ISBN 1-55561-042-0
    1. Entertaining. 2. Menus. 3. Cookery.
I. Hoffman, Gar. II. Title.

TX731.H555   1991
642' .4—dc20   91-15831
                                           CIP

Notice: The information in this book is true
and complete to the best of our knowledge.
It is offered with no guarantees on the part
of the authors or Fisher Books. Authors and
publisher disclaim all liability in connection
with the use of this book.

Table of Contents

About the Authors

Mable and Gar Hoffman, Fisher Books' best-selling cookbook team, have added *Carefree Entertaining* to their long list of successful cookbooks. Their other cookbooks published by Fisher Books include *Ice Cream*, *Frozen Yogurt* and *Crockery Favorites*.

Five of Mable's cookbooks have won R.T. French Tastemaker Awards, the "Oscar" for cookbooks. Although Mable's name appears on most of their books, Gar has been a silent contributor.

Mable and Gar make their home in Southern California, where they are famous for their entertaining skills. Nothing delights them more than inviting family and friends over for planned or impromptu get-togethers.

The Hoffmans own and manage Hoffman Food Consultants, Inc. They concentrate their efforts on food styling, recipe development and writing.

Introduction

Carefree Entertaining is designed for you. Getting together with family and friends is an important pastime, and our make-ahead plan can come to your rescue. Choose menus that appeal to you. Check the timetable and decide what can be made ahead or shortcuts you'll take.

Flexibility is the key to using these menus. Freely substitute your favorite foods for those we've suggested. Be adventurous by mixing and matching dishes from several of our menus. In each recipe we've told you how to prepare ahead, store and complete. We hope you enjoy the versatility of this plan.

Some of our shortcuts suggest purchasing prepared items from the bakery, deli or gourmet shop. These shortcuts are very handy for spur-of-the-moment entertaining.

Planning ensures successful entertaining. After you've decided to entertain, develop a plan of action. Will it be a traditional breakfast, lunch or dinner? Or will you have a brunch, dessert, appetizer buffet or picnic? Will it be casual or formal?

Plan your guest list — Do you like to give intimate dinners? Or do you enjoy bringing together a wide variety of personalities? The number of people you invite determines the type of meal, the menu and equipment needed. Also decide how you'll invite your guests. For informal and spur-of-the-moment occasions, the telephone is the fastest way. Whether you telephone or send a written invitation, let them know the type of event you're planning. This way your guests will come prepared.

Buffet or Sit-Down Meals — By serving buffet-style you can entertain more guests. Attractively arrange food and utensils so guests can help themselves quickly and conveniently. Cut food into individual portions. Set up small tables to encourage guests to get acquainted.

Generally a sit-down dinner is more formal. You'll set the table in a more traditional style. Perk up a table setting by doing something special in the way you fold the napkins. Perhaps you'll want to slip in a fresh flower or use interesting napkin rings.

Let your guests know that you appreciate their presence by making an extra effort to make the table attractive. If fresh flowers are not available, consider a basket of fresh vegetables. Even a grouping of interesting stones, carved figures or a variety of candles can be a showpiece. Small potted plants grouped together can reflect an interest in plants.

Consider entertaining in areas other than the dining room. For casual dining invite your guests into the kitchen. Many times they are eager to help in final preparations and serving, making them feel they are part of the family.

With larger groups, appetizers and drinks served in the living room and den offer an opportunity for you to introduce guests to one another in a relaxed atmosphere.

You may fill individual plates at the table or pass serving dishes. If you have help or don't mind spending extra time in the kitchen, arrange food attractively on plates and bring them to the table ready to be admired and enjoyed. After eating in the dining room, you have the choice of serving dessert there or waiting a short time and serving dessert in another area.

Let the type of party guide you in deciding the location. Take advantage of outdoor facilities in your area where you can host a lovely picnic or brunch. The park or beach provides a perfect setting for gatherings that include children. When moving your party to another location, make a checklist to avoid forgetting a necessary item like matches or fuel for the barbecue.

Deciding on the Menu — The menu depends on the type of party. When selecting foods for holidays or special events, don't be afraid to break tradition. Combine foods that aren't usually served at the same meal. Feature foods from two or more ethnic groups for a lively meal. Be sure to make a shopping list.

Beautifully presented food heightens the appetite. That's why it's important to think about the beauty of your food when planning the menu. Include a variety of textures, colors and shapes as well as compatible or contrasting flavors.

Check each recipe to determine the equipment needed. Are you missing any pans, bowls, trays or platters? If you can't borrow them, check for a place to rent what you need. For a large affair, you'll probably need extra tables, chairs and linens.

Try recipes before serving them. After trying a new recipe, adjust seasonings and cooking method to suit your taste and style. Write down changes on the recipe so you won't forget.

Check with your market, bakery or delicatessen where you plan to purchase food for the party. If meats or produce must be ordered, give them advance notice.

Storing Food — Make maximum use of your freezer and refrigerator. Many foods such as breads, cookies, cakes and certain main dishes may be frozen a month or so before the event.

Be sure food is properly packaged for freezing. Improper packaging results in freezer burn, making food dry and unpalatable. Plastic containers with tight-fitting lids are good for sauces, ice cream and fragile foods that may crush easily. Label and date packages before freezing. Also indicate whether the food is uncooked, partially cooked or ready to eat.

Cover all refrigerated food. Covered food is not likely to impart or absorb odors and flavors from other foods.

If your refrigerator is filled and there's no room for a salad or cold drinks, put ice chests to work. Don't forget to make or purchase extra ice cubes and keep them in an ice chest during the party. If the weather is warm, you'll need more ice.

Heating Food — Microwaving is the fastest and one of the most practical ways to reheat food. Unlike a regular oven, the time needed to heat food in a microwave depends on the quantity, density and shape of the food. Although there's no exact formula for heating time, the microwave will heat most food in about one-fourth the time of a conventional oven.

The broiler and oven are also wonderful for last-minute heating. Prepare a main dish or hot appetizer the day before and put it in the oven just before guests arrive. Broiling seldom takes more than five minutes and produces bubbly hot food.

Here are our favorite ways to keep food hot:

Chafing dishes or fondue pots have been popular with caterers for many years. They are made in a variety of shapes, sizes and materials. Most of them are very attractive.

Hot trays are available in sizes ranging from a small coffee server to the large buffet size that accommodates several serving dishes.

Slow-cookers (Crock-Pot®) are ideal for keeping soups, stews, drinks, dips, meat balls and other foods hot. They also keep foods hot a long time after they're unplugged. For your next picnic, fill a slow-cooker with hot food. Cover, wrap in several layers of newspapers and it's ready to travel.

Electric skillets are great for last-minute cooking or reheating and can be used to keep food warm.

Conventional ovens keep foods like an extra loaf of bread or platter of meat warm. Smaller quantities can be warmed in a toaster oven.

Keep warm foods warm and cold foods cold. Don't leave foods at room temperature more than 2 hours.

Wines and Other Beverages — We have not listed beverages in the menus unless they are unique to the theme.

Not long ago it was considered fashionable, almost mandatory to serve specific wines with specific foods. Today the "right" wine is one that pleases your palate.

Wine and food should complement each other. The wine should not overpower the food and vice versa. Ethnic wines can be served with the same ethnic food.

The temperature at which the wine is served is also an important consideration. We think white and rosé wines are most enjoyable at 50F (10C), red wines at 60F (15C) and sparkling wines at 40F to 45F (5C).

Documentation

Nutrient analysis was calculated using The Food Processor II Nutrition & Diet Analysis System software program, version 3.0, copyright 1988, 1990, by ESHA Research. Analysis does not include optional ingredients. The higher number is used for the range of servings.

Abbreviations

Because words like *carbohydrates* are too long to fit the recipe in chart form, we have abbreviated as follows:

Cal = Calories
Prot = Protein
Carb = Carbohydrates
Chol = Cholesterol

New Year's Eve

❖ *Menu* ❖

Cheese & Jalapeño Spread
Appetizer Cheesecake
Honey-Mustard Ribs
Turkey-Avocado Mousse
Salmon Spectacular
Hazelnut Dream, page 122

Serves 12 to 15.

Timetable:

- Hazelnut Dream – Bake and freeze unfrosted up to 1 month. Glaze thawed cake.
- Honey-Mustard Ribs – Bake and freeze ribs up to 2 weeks. Thaw in refrigerator. Marinate 1 hour; then broil.
- Appetizer Cheesecake, Cheese & Jalapeño Spread and Turkey-Avocado Mousse – Make 24 hours ahead.
- Salmon Spectacular – Poach and refrigerate up to 24 hours. Make garnishes 24 hours ahead; refrigerate. On day of party, make toppings and garnish up to 2 hours ahead.

Shortcuts:

- Omit 1 or 2 dishes.
- Substitute cream cheese for the cheese spread in Cheese & Jalapeño Spread.
- Substitute guacamole dip for Turkey-Avocado Mousse.

Cheese & Jalapeño Spread

Makes about 4 cups.

2 cups shredded Monterey Jack cheese (8 oz.)

1 (8-oz.) pkg. Neufchâtel cheese, room temperature

1 cup cottage cheese, drained

1 teaspoon Worcestershire sauce

1 teaspoon minced green onion

1 teaspoon seasoned salt

1 (10-oz.) jar jalapeño jelly

Assorted crackers

Brush a 5-1/2-cup ring mold with vegetable oil; set aside. In a food processor fitted with a metal blade, combine cheeses, Worcestershire sauce, green onion and seasoned salt. Process until blended. Firmly pack into prepared ring mold. Complete now or make ahead.

To complete now, cover and refrigerate at least 4 hours. To serve, loosen edges from mold with a spatula. Invert onto a serving dish; remove mold. Spoon jelly into a bowl; place in center of mold. Arrange crackers around mold. Guests spread crackers with cheese, then top with jalapeño jelly.

To make ahead, refrigerate covered spread up to 24 hours.

1 tablespoon contains:

Cal	Prot	Carb	Fat	Chol	Sodium
37	2g	3g	2g	6mg	85mg

Give a gala New Year's Eve open house. Feature Salmon Spectacular surrounded with a variety of dishes. Add elegance to the buffet table by placing mirror tiles down the center.

Appetizer Cheesecake

Makes 35 to 40 appetizer servings.

3 cups shredded sharp cheddar cheese (12 oz.)

2 cups cottage cheese, drained

2 tablespoons prepared horseradish

1/2 cup reduced-calorie mayonnaise

2 tablespoons Dijon-style mustard

4 slices Canadian bacon, chopped

1 tablespoon minced fresh chives

1/4 teaspoon salt

1/8 teaspoon pepper

2 tablespoons melted butter

Sliced pitted ripe olives

Pimiento strips

Sliced green onions or radishes

Assorted crackers or sliced French bread

In bowl or food processor fitted with a metal blade, combine cheddar cheese, cottage cheese, horseradish, mayonnaise, mustard, bacon, chives, salt, pepper and butter. Process until blended but not smooth. Press into an ungreased 8-inch springform pan. Complete now or make ahead.

To complete now, cover and refrigerate at least 4 hours. Remove pan. Garnish top with rings of olives, pimiento, green onions or radishes. Slice and serve with crackers or French bread.

To make ahead, cover and refrigerate up to 24 hours. Garnish and serve as directed above.

1 serving contains:

Cal	Prot	Carb	Fat	Chol	Sodium
63	4g	1g	5g	14mg	178mg

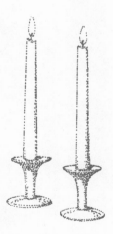

Honey-Mustard Ribs

Makes 12 to 15 appetizer servings.

3 to 3-1/2 lbs. pork spareribs, halved crosswise

1/3 cup Dijon-style mustard

1/3 cup honey

2 tablespoons lemon juice

1/4 cup red-wine vinegar

1/3 cup lightly packed brown sugar

1 tablespoon soy sauce

1 teaspoon salt

1/4 teaspoon pepper

2 tablespoons sesame seeds

Parsley sprigs, if desired

Cut ribs into individual riblets. Place on broiler rack. Cover with foil. Bake at 325F (165C) 1 to 1-1/2 hours or until meat is tender. In a saucepan, combine mustard and honey. Stir in lemon juice, vinegar, brown sugar, soy sauce, salt and pepper. Heat, stirring constantly, until sugar dissolves. Place ribs in a shallow bowl; pour marinade over ribs. Complete now or make ahead.

To complete now, cover and refrigerate 1 hour. Drain ribs and reserve marinade. Broil ribs 5 to 6 inches from heat 2 to 3 minutes, brushing with marinade. Turn; brush with marinade. Broil until browned and crisp. Sprinkle with sesame seeds and garnish with parsley, if desired; serve hot.

To make ahead, cool and cover with foil. Refrigerate overnight or freeze up to 2 weeks. Thaw ribs overnight in refrigerator. Drain and reserve marinade. Broil, garnish and serve ribs as directed above.

1 serving contains:

Cal	Prot	Carb	Fat	Chol	Sodium
174	10g	12g	10g	37mg	311mg

❖ *Dijon-style mustard is a medium-hot mustard that teams well with honey for prizewinning ribs.*

Turkey-Avocado Mousse

Makes about 3 cups or 12 to 15 buffet servings.

1 (1/4-oz.) envelope
    unflavored gelatin

1/2 cup cold water

1/2 cup plain lowfat yogurt

1/2 cup mayonnaise

1 teaspoon seasoned salt

1/4 teaspoon pepper

1/2 teaspoon dried
    marjoram leaves

1 cup chopped cooked
    turkey or chicken

1 avocado, chopped

2 green onions, chopped

2 bacon slices, cooked,
    drained

1/4 cup dry white wine

Fresh vegetables, sliced

Crackers

In a saucepan, combine gelatin and water; let stand 3 minutes. Stir over low heat until gelatin dissolves; set aside. In a bowl, combine yogurt, mayonnaise, seasoned salt, pepper and marjoram; set aside. In a blender or food processor fitted with a metal blade, combine turkey or chicken, avocado, green onions, bacon and wine. Process until chopped but not puréed. Spoon mixture into a bowl. Gradually stir in gelatin. Fold chicken and yogurt mixtures together. Pour into an ungreased 4-cup mold. Complete now or make ahead.

To complete now, cover mousse and refrigerate at least 4 hours. Invert mousse onto a plate. Serve with vegetables or crackers.

To make ahead, cover mousse and refrigerate up to 24 hours. Refrigerate vegetables overnight. Serve as directed above.

1 serving contains:

Cal	Prot	Carb	Fat	Chol	Sodium
104	4g	2g	9g	13mg	211mg

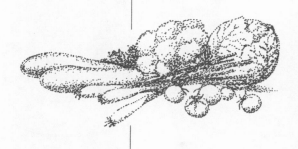

Salmon Spectacular

2-1/2 quarts water

1 cup dry white wine

1 onion, sliced

1 celery stalk with leaves, chopped

2 bay leaves

1 teaspoon salt

1 (2-1/2 to 3-1/2 lb.) dressed whole or half salmon

1/2 unpeeled cucumber, thinly sliced

8 to 10 carrot curls

Fresh Herb Topping:

1/2 cup mayonnaise

1/4 cup dairy sour cream

1/4 cup watercress leaves

1/4 cup chopped fresh parsley

3 tablespoons chopped fresh dill

1 tablespoon chopped green onion

1/4 teaspoon salt

1/8 teaspoon pepper

In a fish poacher or roasting pan, combine water, wine, onion, celery, bay leaves and 1 teaspoon salt. Bring to boil. Measure fish at thickest part. Lay fish on 3 layers of cheesecloth several inches larger than it. Lift salmon into simmering liquid. Cover; simmer 10 minutes for each inch of thickness or until it flakes easily. Lift salmon out and place on platter.

To complete now, refrigerate salmon 2 hours or until cold. Remove fins, skin and vein of dark meat. Garnish with cucumbers and carrots. Serve with Fresh Herb Topping.

To make Fresh Herb Topping, combine mayonnaise, sour cream, watercress, parsley, dill, green onion, 1/4 teaspoon salt and pepper in blender or food processor. Process until mixture is combined.

To make ahead, refrigerate cooked salmon up to 24 hours. Prepare Fresh Herb Topping 2 hours ahead. Complete as directed above.

1 serving contains:

Cal	Prot	Carb	Fat	Chol	Sodium
168	16g	3g	9g	45mg	280mg

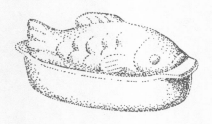

Emerald-Isle Feast

Leprechaun Soup
Erin Cabbage Rolls
Spicy Brown Mustard
Killarney Potato Balls
Calico Rolls
Emerald-Isle Sorbet
Irish Coffee

Serves 6.

Timetable:

- Spicy Brown Mustard – Make up to 7 days ahead.
- Emerald-Isle Sorbet – Make 3 to 4 days ahead. Allow 3 to 4 hours to freeze, beat and freeze again.
- Erin Cabbage Rolls – Make 24 hours ahead.
- Calico Rolls – Make 24 hours ahead.
- Leprechaun Soup – Make 24 hours ahead.
- Killarney Potato Balls – Cook potatoes and shape balls 24 hours ahead. Bake 15 to 20 minutes before serving.
- Irish Coffee – Make coffee before guests arrive.

Shortcuts:

- Purchase spicy mustard instead of making it.
- Serve commercial sherbet or sorbet instead of Emerald-Isle Sorbet.
- Serve regular coffee instead of Irish Coffee.

Leprechaun Soup

**2 tablespoons butter or
margarine**

**1/4 cup chopped green
onions**

**2 medium potatoes, peeled,
diced**

**5 cups chicken broth or
bouillon**

1/2 lb. Chinese pea pods

**1/2 cup plain lowfat
yogurt, stirred**

**1 (8-oz.) can sliced water
chestnuts, drained**

1/2 teaspoon salt

1/8 teaspoon pepper

1/4 teaspoon ground ginger

1/8 teaspoon dry mustard

Sliced green onions

In a 2-quart saucepan, melt butter or margarine.
Add chopped green onions; sauté until soft. Add
potatoes and broth or bouillon. Cover; simmer
20 minutes or until potatoes are tender. Purée
1/2 at a time in blender or food processor.
Remove stems from pea pods; cut each pod into
4 or 5 pieces; set aside. Stir 2 tablespoons purée
into yogurt. Then add yogurt to remaining
potatoes. Stir in pea pods, water chestnuts, salt,
pepper, ginger and dry mustard. Over medium
heat, bring to boil. Complete now or make ahead.

To complete now, pour into individual bowls.
Garnish with sliced green onions.

To make ahead, cover and refrigerate up to
24 hours. Reheat and serve as directed above.

1 serving contains:

Cal	Prot	Carb	Fat	Chol	Sodium
154	7g	19g	5g	12mg	231mg

*Enjoy a family meal celebrating St. Patrick's
Day with an exciting new version of
traditional corned beef and cabbage. Pots
of shamrocks on the table help celebrate the
occasion.*

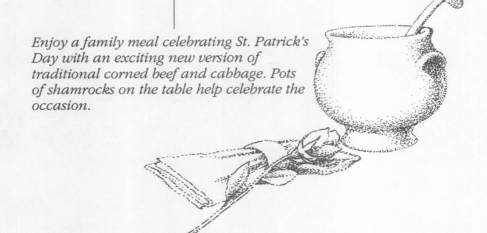

Makes 10 cabbage rolls.

1 large cabbage

1 lb. cooked corned beef, coarsely chopped

1 medium onion, quartered

1 stalk celery, cut into 1-inch pieces

1 egg, beaten slightly

1 cup cooked brown rice

2 teaspoons Spicy Brown Mustard, page 10

1 cube beef bouillon

1/4 cup boiling water

1 (12-oz.) can beer

1 tablespoon vegetable oil

1 tablespoon flour

Remove 10 outside leaves of cabbage. Cut and remove thick core of each leaf. Blanch leaves in boiling water about 1 minute or until limp; drain. Finely chop cooked corned beef in food processor. Remove meat and process onion and celery until finely chopped. In bowl, combine egg, cooked rice, mustard, corned beef, onion and celery. Spoon about 1/2 cup corned-beef mixture on rib end of each cabbage leaf. Roll up; tuck in ends. Arrange, seam-side down in 13" x 9" baking pan. Preheat oven to 375F (190C). Dissolve bouillon in boiling water; combine with beer in bowl. Pour over stuffed cabbage and cover. Bake about 1 hour or until tender. Heat oil in skillet; stir in flour; then 1 cup broth from baked cabbage rolls. Stir until thickened.

To complete now, arrange cabbage rolls on platter; spoon sauce over all. Serve hot with Spicy Brown Mustard.

To make ahead, cover cooked rolls and refrigerate up to 24 hours. Reheat and serve as directed above.

1 roll contains:

Cal	Prot	Carb	Fat	Chol	Sodium
188	14g	10g	9g	60mg	490mg

❖ *The beef bouillon and beer combine to enhance the traditional flavor of this homey dish.*

Makes about 2/3 cup.

**2 tablespoons mustard
seeds**

1/4 cup red-wine vinegar

1/4 cup dry red wine

2 tablespoons dry mustard

1/4 cup water

**1 teaspoon prepared
horseradish**

**1/8 teaspoon ground
turmeric**

1/8 teaspoon ground cloves

1 tablespoon brown sugar

In a blender, combine mustard seeds and vinegar. Process until seeds are partially crushed and form a paste. Let stand 5 minutes. In a saucepan, combine wine, dry mustard, water, horseradish, turmeric, cloves, brown sugar and vinegar mixture. Stirring constantly, cook over low heat 6 to 8 minutes or until thickened. Set aside to cool. Complete now or make ahead.

To complete now, cover and let flavors blend at least 2 hours.

To make ahead, cover and refrigerate up to 7 days.

1 tablespoon contains:

Cal	Prot	Carb	Fat	Chol	Sodium
10	0	2g	0	0	1mg

10

Killarney Potato Balls

Makes 6 servings.

6 medium boiling potatoes, peeled

2 tablespoons butter or margarine

1/4 cup dairy sour cream

1/2 teaspoon salt

1/8 teaspoon pepper

1 egg

1 tablespoon minced green onion

1 tablespoon minced fresh parsley

2 tablespoons butter or margarine, melted

1/4 cup grated Parmesan cheese

Parsley sprigs

Boil potatoes until tender. Drain; mash until smooth. Beat in 2 tablespoons butter or margarine, sour cream, salt, pepper, egg, green onion and parsley. Shape into 12 (2-inch) balls. Complete now or make ahead.

To complete now, refrigerate at least 2 hours. Preheat oven to 375F (190C). Place potato balls in an ungreased 13" x 9" baking pan. Brush with melted butter or margarine; sprinkle with Parmesan cheese. Bake 15 to 20 minutes or until lightly browned. Spoon into a serving bowl. Garnish with parsley sprigs.

To make ahead, refrigerate up to 24 hours. Bake and serve as directed above.

1 serving contains:

Cal	Prot	Carb	Fat	Chol	Sodium
236	5g	28g	12g	63mg	327mg

Calico Rolls

Makes 6 servings.

3/4 cup shredded cheddar cheese (3 oz.)

3 tablespoons butter or margarine, room temperature

1/3 cup chopped pitted ripe olives

1/4 cup chopped green bell pepper

2 tablespoons chopped pimiento

3 (6-inch) French rolls, cut in half lengthwise

Shamrock Garnishes:
2 large green bell peppers

In a bowl, combine cheese, butter or margarine, olives, bell pepper and pimiento. Spread mixture on cut sides of rolls. Place cut-side up in an ungreased shallow baking pan. Complete now or make ahead.

To complete now, prepare Shamrock Garnishes; preheat broiler. Broil rolls about 5 inches from heat until cheese melts. Top each roll with a shamrock garnish; arrange rolls on a serving plate. Serve warm.

To make Shamrock Garnishes, draw a 1-1/2- to 2-inch shamrock design. Using pattern, cut 6 shamrocks from green peppers. Refrigerate shamrocks in a plastic bag until served.

To make ahead, cover rolls and refrigerate 24 hours. Broil, garnish and serve as directed above.

1 serving contains:

Cal	Prot	Carb	Fat	Chol	Sodium
223	7g	20g	13g	30mg	391mg

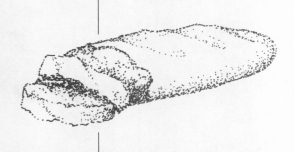

Emerald-Isle Sorbet

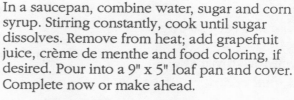

Makes about 1 quart.

1 cup water
3/4 cup sugar
1/4 cup light corn syrup
2 cups grapefruit juice
1/4 cup green crème de menthe liqueur
3 or 4 drops green food coloring, if desired

In a saucepan, combine water, sugar and corn syrup. Stirring constantly, cook until sugar dissolves. Remove from heat; add grapefruit juice, crème de menthe and food coloring, if desired. Pour into a 9" x 5" loaf pan and cover. Complete now or make ahead.

To complete now, place in freezer until almost firm, 1 to 3 hours. Break mixture into small pieces. In a chilled bowl, blender or food processor fitted with a metal blade, process until smooth and fluffy but not thawed. Return mixture to pan; freeze until firm, 1 to 3 hours. For a smoother texture, beat mixture a second time; freeze until served. Spoon or scoop into balls. Serve in individual dessert dishes.

To make ahead, freeze up to 4 days. Break frozen mixture into small pieces. In a chilled bowl, blender or food processor fitted with a metal blade, process as directed above.

1 serving contains:

Cal	Prot	Carb	Fat	Chol	Sodium
155	0	35g	0	0	6mg

Irish Coffee

2 tablespoons sugar
5 cups hot very strong coffee
1/2 cup Irish whiskey
Whipped cream

Spoon 1 teaspoon sugar into each of 6 Irish-coffee glasses or cups. Pour about 1 tablespoon hot coffee into each glass or cup. Stir until sugar dissolves. Add hot coffee until at least 3/4 full. Add about 1-1/2 tablespoons whiskey to each. Top with a dollop of whipped cream. Serve hot.

1 serving contains:

Cal	Prot	Carb	Fat	Chol	Sodium
60	0	5g	0	0	5mg

Easter Celebration

❖ *Menu* ❖

Cheese & Sausage Pouches
Pork Loin with Herbs
Roasted New Potatoes
Carrots Siam
Spiced Zucchini Sticks
Jalapeño Spirals
Double-Almond Easter Cake

Serves 8.

Timetable:

- Cheese & Sausage Pouches – Make and freeze up to 3 weeks ahead. Thaw pouches in refrigerator overnight, or bake and refrigerate up to 24 hours.
- Spiced Zucchini Sticks – Make up to 7 days ahead.
- Double-Almond Easter Cake – Make up to 24 hours ahead; cover and store at room temperature.
- Jalapeño Spirals – Refrigerate shaped rolls up to 24 hours. 1-1/2 hours before serving, remove from refrigerator.
- Pork Loin with Herbs – Cover roast with herbs up to 24 hours ahead.
- Carrots Siam – Steam or cook up to 12 hours.
- Roasted New Potatoes – Roast with pork loin.

Shortcuts:

- Cook and serve commercially frozen buttered carrots.
- Steam zucchini; omit spices.

Cheese & Sausage Pouches

Makes 22 appetizers.

1/4 lb. hot and spicy bulk pork sausage, crumbled

1 egg, lightly beaten

1 cup cottage cheese

2 teaspoons minced fresh chives

2 tablespoons grated Parmesan cheese

22 round won-ton skins or potsticker wrappers

1 tablespoon melted butter

In skillet, brown sausage; drain thoroughly. In bowl, combine egg, cottage cheese, chives, cooked sausage and Parmesan cheese. Preheat oven to 400F (205C). Spoon 1 tablespoon mixture into center of each won-ton skin. Pull up sides and pleat. Brush with melted butter. Place on a baking sheet. Bake 10 minutes or until light brown.

To complete now, arrange on serving tray. Serve warm.

To make ahead, cool, cover and refrigerate overnight or freeze up to 3 weeks. To reheat, thaw and remove cover. Preheat oven to 375F (190C). Heat 8 to 10 minutes or until warm.

1 appetizer contains:

Cal	Prot	Carb	Fat	Chol	Sodium
44	3g	1g	3g	15mg	92mg

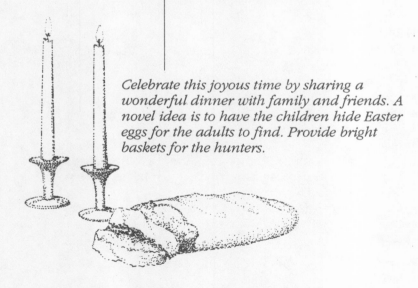

Celebrate this joyous time by sharing a wonderful dinner with family and friends. A novel idea is to have the children hide Easter eggs for the adults to find. Provide bright baskets for the hunters.

16

Pork Loin with Herbs

Makes 8 or 9 servings.

**1 (5-1/2- to 6-lb.) pork-loin
center-rib roast,
backbone removed**

1/2 teaspoon salt

1/4 teaspoon pepper

**1/4 cup chopped fresh
sage or 1 teaspoon dried
sage**

**1 tablespoon chopped
fresh marjoram leaves
or 1/4 teaspoon dried-
leaf marjoram**

**1/4 cup chopped celery
leaves**

**1/2 cup apple cider or
apple juice**

Cut a 24" x 18" piece of heavy foil. Place roast,
fat-side up, in center of foil. Sprinkle roast with
salt and pepper. Combine sage, marjoram and
celery leaves; pat herbs over fat. Fold foil over
roast; crimp or fold edges together. Complete
now or make ahead.

To complete now, place wrapped roast in a
roasting pan. Roast at 325F (165C) 1 hour.
Open foil; spoon apple cider or juice over roast.
Continue roasting 1-1/2 to 2 hours longer or until
a meat thermometer registers 170F (75C). To
serve, cut between ribs. Spoon juice over each
serving. Serve hot.

To make ahead, refrigerate foil-wrapped roast
up to 24 hours. Roast and serve as directed above.

1 serving contains:

Cal	Prot	Carb	Fat	Chol	Sodium
626	75g	2g	33g	239mg	291mg

Carrots Siam

Makes 6 to 8 servings.

**8 large carrots, peeled, or
2 (10-oz.) pkgs. frozen
baby carrots**

**2 tablespoons butter or
margarine**

**2 tablespoons fruit
chutney, finely chopped**

1/4 teaspoon ground ginger

Cut carrots into julienne pieces. Steam or cook carrots in lightly salted water until tender; drain. Complete now or make ahead.

To complete now, melt butter or margarine in skillet. Stir in chutney and ginger. Add cooked carrots. Stirring frequently, cook until hot and glazed.

To make ahead, cool carrots under running water to prevent overcooking. Cover and refrigerate overnight. Glaze as directed above.

1 serving contains:

Cal	Prot	Carb	Fat	Chol	Sodium
61	1g	9g	3g	8mg	97mg

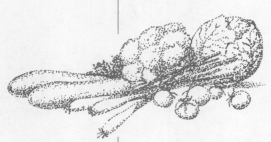

❖ *A simple way to lift everyday carrots out of the doldrums by adding a tangy chutney sauce.*

Spiced Zucchini Sticks

Makes about 3 cups.

2 tablespoons salt

3 medium zucchini, each cut lengthwise into 8 strips

1 onion, sliced

1-1/2 cups cider vinegar

3/4 cup sugar

1/4 teaspoon ground turmeric

1/2 teaspoon celery seeds

1/2 teaspoon whole mixed pickling spices

In a bowl, stir salt into 1 quart water until dissolved. Add zucchini and onion. Cover and let stand at least 2 hours. Drain. In a 2-quart pan, combine vinegar, sugar, turmeric, celery seeds and pickling spices. Bring to a boil; add drained zucchini and onion. Simmer 2 to 3 minutes or until zucchini is tender-crisp. Cool in liquid. Complete now or make ahead.

To complete now, drain; serve zucchini strips and onions in a serving bowl.

To make ahead, cover and refrigerate cooked zucchini and liquid up to 7 days. Drain and serve as directed above.

1 tablespoon contains:

Cal	Prot	Carb	Fat	Chol	Sodium
15	0	4g	0	0	267mg

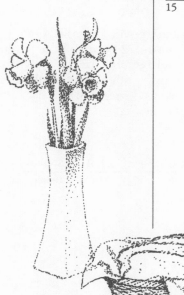

Jalapeño Spirals

Makes 10 rolls.

1 (1/4-oz.) pkg. active dry yeast

1/4 cup warm water (110F, 45C)

1/4 cup warm milk (110F, 45C)

2 tablespoons sugar

3 tablespoons butter or margarine, room temperature

1/2 teaspoon salt

1 egg

1-1/2 to 2 cups all-purpose flour

2 (3-oz.) pkgs. cream cheese, room temperature

1/4 cup jalapeño jelly

In a bowl, soften yeast in water. Stir in milk, sugar, butter or margarine, salt, egg and 1 cup flour. Beat until smooth. Stir in enough flour to make a soft dough. Turn out onto a lightly floured surface; knead until smooth and elastic. Place dough in a greased bowl, turning to coat all sides. Cover; let rise in a warm place until doubled. Grease a round 9-inch cake pan. Punch down dough. On a lightly floured surface, roll out to 15" x 9". Spread with cream cheese to 1 inch from edge; then spread with jalapeño jelly. Starting on a long edge, roll up dough, jelly-roll style. Pinch seam to seal; cut roll into 10 slices. Arrange cut-side down in prepared pan. Complete now or make ahead.

To complete now, cover; let rise in a warm place until doubled. Preheat oven to 375F (190C). Bake 25 minutes or until lightly browned. Serve warm on a platter.

To make ahead, cover and refrigerate up to 24 hours. About 1-1/2 hours before serving, remove from refrigerator. Let stand covered at room temperature until almost doubled in bulk. Bake and serve as directed above.

1 roll contains:

Cal	Prot	Carb	Fat	Chol	Sodium
200	4g	23g	10g	50mg	198mg

❖ *Jalapeño jelly provides an accent to this creamy filled roll.*

Double-Almond Easter Cake

Makes 1 (10-inch) cake.

3/4 cup butter or margarine, room temperature

1 (7-oz.) pkg. almond paste, crumbled

1-1/2 cups sugar

6 eggs

1/4 teaspoon salt

1/2 teaspoon baking soda

3 cups all-purpose flour

1/2 cup dairy sour cream

2 tablespoons almond-flavored liqueur

Glaze:

1-1/2 cups sifted powdered sugar

1 tablespoon almond-flavored liqueur

1 tablespoon lemon juice

1 tablespoon butter, melted

2 to 3 tablespoons milk

25 pastel-colored candy-coated almonds

Preheat oven to 325F (165C). Grease and flour a 10-inch tube pan; set aside. In a mixer bowl, beat butter or margarine and almond paste until smooth. Add sugar; beat until fluffy. Beat in eggs, 1 at a time, beating well after each addition. Beat in salt and baking soda. Stir in flour alternately with sour cream; beat until smooth. Stir in liqueur. Spoon into prepared pan. Bake 70 minutes or until a wooden pick inserted in center comes out clean. Let stand 15 minutes. Loosen cake from pan with a spatula. Invert onto a rack; remove pan. Let cool. Prepare glaze. Lightly spread glaze on top and side of cake. Before glaze sets, arrange 5 clusters of 5 almonds each on top to resemble flowers. Complete now or make ahead.

To make Glaze, in a bowl, combine powdered sugar, liqueur, lemon juice, butter and milk. If mixture is too thick, thin with a few drops of milk.

To complete now, after glaze sets, cut into wedges to serve.

To make ahead, cover decorated cake. Store at room temperature up to 24 hours.

1 serving contains:

Cal	Prot	Carb	Fat	Chol	Sodium
527	9g	72g	23g	145mg	224mg

Mother's Day Brunch

❖ *Menu* ❖

Mom's Eye-Opener
French-Toast Supreme
Homemade Sausage
Fresh Strawberry Treat
Touch-of-Gold Cookies

Serves 6.

Timetable:

- Touch-of-Gold Cookies – Make and freeze up to 1 month.
- Mom's Eye-Opener – Make basic mixture up to 2 days ahead. Add tomato juice before serving.
- Homemade Sausage – Make up to 24 hours ahead; partially cook.
- French-Toast Supreme – Make up to 24 hours ahead.
- Fresh Strawberry Treat – Purchase strawberries 1 day ahead. Refrigerate until serving time.

Shortcuts:

- Buy links or bulk pork sausage.
- Make regular French toast.

Mom's Eye-Opener

1/2 cup chopped celery

2 tablespoons chopped onion

2 tablespoons chopped parsley

2 (10-1/2-oz.) cans condensed beef broth, undiluted

1/4 teaspoon salt

1/8 teaspoon seasoned pepper

4 cups tomato juice

Celery stalks

In a saucepan, combine celery, onion, parsley, broth, salt and pepper. Bring to a boil; reduce heat. Simmer 10 minutes. Purée in blender or food processor fitted with a metal blade. Line a sieve with 2 thicknesses of cheesecloth. Pour purée through lined sieve into a pitcher. Discard vegetables. Stir tomato juice into purée. Complete now or make ahead.

To complete now, pour into a saucepan. Stir occasionally over medium heat until warmed through. Pour into mugs; serve warm with celery-stalk stirrers. To serve cold, chill in refrigerator; serve in drinking glasses.

To make ahead, cover and refrigerate up to 3 days. Serve warm or cold as directed above.

1 serving contains:

Cal	Prot	Carb	Fat	Chol	Sodium
32	2g	7g	0	0	588mg

The perfect occasion for a patio brunch. Simple foods served with style. Add additional flare to French-Toast Supreme by sprinkling fresh blueberries or raspberries over orange sections.

French-Toast Supreme

Makes 6 servings.

1/2 (16-oz.) loaf French bread or 1 (8-oz.) baguette

4 eggs

1/3 cup orange juice

1/2 teaspoon grated orange peel

1-1/4 cups milk

2 tablespoons butter or margarine, melted

1/8 teaspoon ground cinnamon

2 tablespoons brown sugar

Mandarin-orange sections

Maple syrup or honey, if desired

Cut bread in half horizontally. Starting at cut surfaces, cut in 1-inch slices, almost to bottom crust. Leave a small amount of crust at bottom uncut to hold it together. Place both halves, cut-side up, in an ungreased 13" x 9" baking dish; set aside. In a bowl, beat eggs; stir in orange juice, orange peel, milk and butter or margarine. Spoon over bread. Let stand 5 minutes. Turn cut-side down. In a bowl, combine cinnamon and brown sugar. Sprinkle cinnamon mixture over bread and cover. Complete now or make ahead.

To complete now, refrigerate at least 2 hours. Preheat oven to 325F (165C). Bake uncovered 30 to 40 minutes or until golden brown and firm. To serve, cut slices apart; arrange on a serving plate. Garnish with orange sections; serve hot with maple syrup or honey, if desired.

To make ahead, refrigerate up to 24 hours. Bake, garnish and serve as directed above.

1 serving contains:

Cal	Prot	Carb	Fat	Chol	Sodium
241	10g	28g	10g	157mg	320mg

Homemade Sausage

Makes 6 servings.

1-1/4 lbs. boneless pork shoulder or leg, cubed

1 medium potato, peeled, cooked, diced

1/2 teaspoon salt

1/2 teaspoon pepper

3/4 teaspoon ground sage

1/4 teaspoon dried-leaf thyme

1/4 teaspoon ground nutmeg

1 tablespoon minced fresh chives

1 tablespoon vegetable oil

In a food processor fitted with a metal blade, combine 1/2 of pork and potato. Process until mixture has texture of ground meat. Remove to a bowl. Repeat with remaining pork and potato. Stir in salt, pepper, sage, thyme, nutmeg and chives. Cover and refrigerate at least 6 hours. Complete now or make ahead.

To complete now, shape sausage into 6 (3-inch) patties. In a skillet, heat vegetable oil. Add sausage; cook until done. Serve immediately.

To make ahead, shape sausage mixture into 6 (3-inch) patties. In a skillet heat vegetable oil. Add patties, lightly brown on both sides; do not cook completely. Cover and refrigerate up to 24 hours. Preheat oven to 325F (165C). Place patties in single layer in ungreased baking pan. Cover with foil. Bake 10 to 15 minutes or until done.

1 serving contains:

Cal	Prot	Carb	Fat	Chol	Sodium
181	19g	5g	9g	64mg	237mg

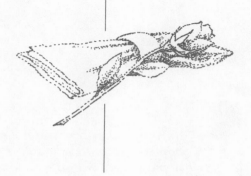

Makes 6 servings.

**2 pints jumbo strawberries
with stems**

1/2 cup dairy sour cream

**1/2 cup lightly packed
brown sugar**

Rinse strawberries; *do not remove stems.* Drain on paper towels until dry. Complete now or make ahead.

To complete now, spoon sour cream and brown sugar into separate bowls. Use a fork to fluff brown sugar. Dip strawberries in sour cream, then in brown sugar.

To make ahead, place a layer of damp towels in container with a tight-fitting lid. Alternate layers of strawberries and damp towels. Cover and refrigerate up to 24 hours. Serve as directed above.

1 serving contains:

Cal	Prot	Carb	Fat	Chol	Sodium
139	1g	26g	4g	9mg	20mg

❖ *If fresh strawberries are not available, cut bananas or pineapple into 1-inch pieces. Apple wedges can also be used.*

Touch-of-Gold Cookies

Makes 50 to 55 cookies.

1 cup corn-oil margarine

3/4 cup sugar

2 eggs

2 cups all-purpose flour

2 teaspoons baking powder

1/2 teaspoon salt

1 cup grated carrots (3 medium)

1/3 cup chopped walnuts

Orange Frosting:

1-3/4 cups sifted powdered sugar

2-1/2 tablespoons orange juice

2 tablespoons butter or margarine, room temperature

3 tablespoons crystallized ginger, finely chopped, for garnish

Preheat oven to 375F (190C). In a bowl, cream margarine; gradually beat in sugar. Add eggs; beat until smooth. In a bowl, combine flour, baking powder and salt. Add to egg mixture; beat until smooth. Stir in carrots and walnuts. Drop dough by heaping teaspoons, 2 inches apart, on ungreased baking sheet. Bake 10 to 12 minutes or until golden brown. Remove and cool. Complete now or make ahead.

To complete now, prepare frosting. Dip tops of cookies into frosting; sprinkle with candied ginger.

To make Orange Frosting, in bowl, combine powdered sugar, orange juice and butter or margarine; beat until fluffy.

To make ahead, freeze unfrosted cookies up to 1 month. Thaw and frost as directed above.

1 cookie contains:

Cal	Prot	Carb	Fat	Chol	Sodium
89	1g	10g	5g	9mg	38mg

Father's Day Picnic

❖ *Menu* ❖

Smoked-Albacore Spread
Picnic Steak
Smoky Baked Limas
Zucchini-Mushroom Salad
Chocolate-Swirl Cake

Serves 6.

Timetable:

- Chocolate-Swirl Cake – Make 1 to 2 days ahead.
- Picnic Steak – Marinate up to 24 hours; prepare onion sauce 2 to 3 hours before serving. Heat sauce and rolls on grill.
- Smoky Baked Limas – Soak, simmer and season up to 24 hours ahead. Bake before picnic.
- Zucchini-Mushroom Salad – Make up to 24 hours ahead.
- Smoked-Albacore Spread – Make up to 24 hours ahead.

Shortcuts:

- Purchase a cake.
- Barbecue plain steak without marinade and onions.

Smoked-Albacore Spread

Makes about 1-1/2 cups.

1/2 lb. dry-smoked albacore or salmon

1/4 cup butter, room temperature

1 tablespoon lemon juice

3/4 teaspoon dried dill weed

1/8 teaspoon pepper

1 tablespoon minced fresh chives

1/3 cup plain lowfat yogurt

Crackers or Melba toast

Remove any skin or bones from fish; cut into 1-inch pieces. In a blender or food processor, combine fish, butter, lemon juice, dill weed, pepper, chives and yogurt. Process until smooth. Spoon into a bowl.

To complete now, cover and carry to picnic in a cooler. To serve, spread on crackers or Melba toast.

To make ahead, cover and refrigerate up to 24 hours. Transport and serve as directed above.

1 tablespoon contains:

Cal	Prot	Carb	Fat	Chol	Sodium
30	2g	0	2g	8mg	92mg

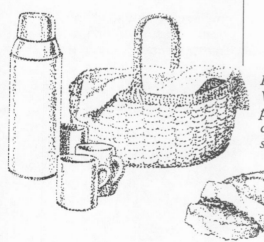

Help dad relax and enjoy a day outdoors. Whether you picnic on the patio or in the park, the grill is perfect for quick outdoor cooking. If you leave home, take barbecue supplies, a board and a sharp knife.

Picnic Steak

Makes 6 servings.

1/2 cup dry red wine

1 garlic clove, crushed

1/4 cup vegetable oil

1/2 teaspoon ground ginger

2 tablespoons soy sauce

1/4 teaspoon salt

1/8 teaspoon pepper

**1 (3-lb.) boneless
  top-sirloin steak (about
  2 inches thick)**

**2 tablespoons butter or
  margarine**

2 onions, thinly sliced

**1 cup beef broth or
  bouillon**

6 French rolls

Butter or margarine

In an 11" x 7" dish or container with a tight-fitting lid, combine red wine, garlic, oil, ginger, soy sauce, salt and pepper. Add steak; spoon sauce over steak. Complete now or make ahead.

To complete now, cover and refrigerate at least 4 hours. Before going to picnic, drain steak; reserve marinade. In a skillet, melt 2 tablespoons butter or margarine. Add onions; sauté until soft. Stir in reserved marinade and broth or bouillon; cook over medium-high heat 5 minutes. Let cool slightly; pour into 4- or 6-cup container with a tight-fitting lid. Cut rolls in half and butter; wrap in foil. Transport meat in an ice chest. At picnic, heat onion sauce. Broil steak about 4 inches from heat 10 minutes on each side until done. Heat foil-wrapped rolls during final 10 minutes steak is cooking. Slice meat; place in hot open-face rolls and top with onion sauce.

To make ahead, cover; refrigerate steak in marinade up to 24 hours. Prepare onion sauce up to 3 hours ahead. Transport, cook and serve as directed above.

1 serving contains:

Cal	Prot	Carb	Fat	Chol	Sodium
699	62g	40g	29g	145mg	967mg

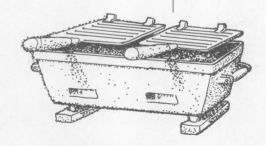

Smoky Baked Limas

Makes 6 to 8 servings.

1 lb. dried small lima beans

1 large onion, chopped

1/2 lb. smoked sausage

1/4 cup lightly packed brown sugar

2 tablespoons Dijon-style mustard

1 teaspoon Worcestershire sauce

1 garlic clove, crushed

1/4 cup molasses

1/4 cup ketchup

1/8 teaspoon ground cloves

1 teaspoon salt

1/8 teaspoon pepper

In a 4-quart saucepan, combine beans and 2 quarts water; boil 2 minutes. Remove from heat; cover and let stand 1 hour. Add onion; bring to a boil; cover. Reduce heat; simmer 1 to 1-1/4 hours until tender. Cut several slices smoked sausage; set aside. Dice remaining sausage. Drain beans, reserving liquid. In a nonmetal casserole, combine diced sausage, brown sugar, mustard, Worcestershire sauce, garlic, molasses, ketchup, cloves, salt and pepper. Stir in drained, cooked beans. Complete now or make ahead.

To complete now, bake at 300F (150C) 1-1/2 to 2 hours, adding reserved bean liquid as needed. Garnish with reserved sliced sausage. To transport to picnic, cover casserole. Wrap with 5 or 6 layers of newspaper, if desired. Or pour beans into a slow-cooker and cover. Wrap in newspaper to transport.

To make ahead, do not bake. Refrigerate reserved liquid and bean mixture separately up to 24 hours. About 2 hours before serving, remove cover from bean mixture; stir. Bake beans as directed above, adding reserved liquid as needed.

1 serving contains:

Cal	Prot	Carb	Fat	Chol	Sodium
258	11g	38g	8g	16mg	656mg

Zucchini-Mushroom Salad

Makes 6 or 7 servings.

2 tablespoons vegetable oil

1 lb. zucchini, cut in 1/4-inch pieces

1/4 cup chopped onion

1 garlic clove, crushed

1/2 lb. mushrooms (about 20 medium), sliced

1/3 cup vinegar

1 tablespoon sugar

1 teaspoon chopped fresh thyme

1 teaspoon chopped fresh oregano

1 tablespoon chopped fresh parsley

1/3 cup dairy sour cream

1/4 cup grated Parmesan cheese

1/4 teaspoon salt

In skillet, heat oil. Add zucchini, onion and garlic. Sauté until zucchini is crisp-tender. Add mushrooms; simmer 1 to 2 minutes; remove from heat. In bowl, combine vinegar, sugar, thyme, oregano and parsley; stir until sugar dissolves. Add sautéed vegetables; toss to coat.

To complete now, refrigerate 3 to 4 hours. Drain, reserving 2 tablespoons liquid in a bowl. Stir in sour cream, Parmesan cheese and salt. Pour over chilled vegetables. Cover; transport in ice chest. To serve, toss well.

To make ahead, refrigerate up to 24 hours. Drain; prepare sour-cream dressing; serve as directed above.

1 serving contains:

Cal	Prot	Carb	Fat	Chol	Sodium
100	3g	7g	7g	7mg	139mg

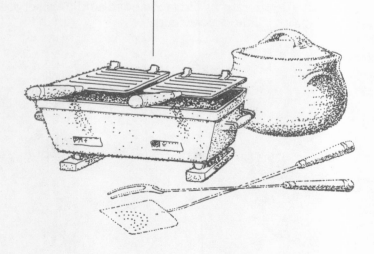

Chocolate-Swirl Cake

Makes 1 (9-inch) 2-layer cake.

3 oz. semi-sweet chocolate

1-3/4 cups all-purpose flour

1 cup granulated sugar

1/2 cup lightly packed brown sugar

1-1/2 teaspoons baking soda

1/2 teaspoon salt

1-1/4 cups buttermilk

1/2 cup vegetable shortening

2 eggs

1 teaspoon vanilla extract

1/4 cup chunk-style peanut butter

Fudge Frosting:

4 oz. semi-sweet chocolate

1 lb. powdered sugar, sifted

1/2 cup butter or margarine, melted

1 teaspoon vanilla extract

1/4 cup milk

1/2 cup chopped peanuts

Melt chocolate; set aside. Grease and flour 2 (9-inch) round cake pans; set aside. Preheat oven to 350F (175C). In a mixer bowl, combine remaining cake ingredients except peanut butter. Beat on low 1/2 minute; then at medium for 3 minutes. Pour 1-1/2 cups batter in a bowl; beat in peanut butter. Add melted chocolate to remaining batter in mixer bowl. Pour 1/2 chocolate batter into each pan. Spoon peanut-butter batter in mounds on chocolate. Make a zig-zag pattern for a marbled effect. Bake 30 to 35 minutes or until wooden pick inserted in center of cake comes out clean. Cool in pans on rack 10 minutes; turn out on rack. Cool. Complete now or make ahead

To complete now, prepare Fudge Frosting; spread about 1/3 of frosting between layers; remaining on top and sides. Sprinkle with peanuts.

To make Fudge Frosting, melt chocolate. In bowl, combine powdered sugar, butter or margarine, vanilla, milk and melted chocolate. Beat until smooth.

To make ahead, freeze unfrosted cake up to 2 weeks. Or make and frost cake 1 or 2 days ahead. Store covered at room temperature.

1 serving contains:

Cal	Prot	Carb	Fat	Chol	Sodium
629	8g	90g	29g	58mg	330mg

❖ *Personalize the cake by spelling DAD with chopped peanuts. Place in a cake carrier for easy transporting.*

Trick-or-Treat Party

❖ *Menu* ❖

Goblin's Drumsticks
Banana-Orange Cups
Jack-O'-Lantern Cookies
Bewitching Gorp
Fresh Apples
Apple Cider

Serves 10 to 12.

Timetable:

- Bewitching Gorp – Make up to 7 days ahead.
- Jack-O'-Lantern Cookies – Make dough up to 2 weeks ahead; freeze. Bake cookies up to 3 days ahead.
- Banana-Orange Cups – Make up to 24 hours ahead; refrigerate.
- Goblin's Drumsticks – Bake up to 24 hours ahead; refrigerate.

Shortcuts:

- Purchase cooked drumsticks.
- Serve commercial granola or trail mix.
- Limit refreshments to Jack-O'-Lantern Cookies and Apple Cider.

Goblin's Drumsticks

Makes 12 drumsticks.

**1-1/2 cups finely crushed
    nacho-cheese-flavored
    corn chips (about 6 oz.)**
1 egg, lightly beaten
1/2 cup milk
12 chicken legs

Grease a 13" x 9" baking pan. Preheat oven to 350F (175C). Pour chips into a pie pan. In a shallow bowl, combine egg and milk. Dip chicken in egg mixture; then in chips. Place in a single layer in greased pan. Bake 45 minutes. Cool in pan 5 minutes. Place chicken on a platter. Refrigerate 30 minutes or until cold. Complete now or make ahead.

To complete now, wrap individually in plastic wrap. Place 1 drumstick in each treat box. Refrigerate until guests arrive.

To make ahead, cover and refrigerate chicken up to 24 hours. Wrap and serve as directed above.

1 serving contains:

Cal	Prot	Carb	Fat	Chol	Sodium
165	14g	9g	8g	60mg	168mg

Present each youngster with a treat box gaily decorated with Halloween designs and filled with a finger-food supper. Share extra Jack-O'-Lantern Cookies with trick-or-treaters who ring your doorbell.

Banana-Orange Cups

Makes 10 to 12 servings.

**1 (6-oz.) pkg.
    orange-flavored gelatin**
2 cups boiling water
2 bananas
1 cup plain yogurt

In a bowl, dissolve gelatin in boiling water. In a bowl, mash 1 banana; stir in yogurt. Gradually stir dissolved gelatin into yogurt mixture. Pour into 10 to 12 (5- or 6-ounce) individual paper cups. Cover cups with lids or foil. Complete now or make ahead.

To complete now, refrigerate until firm. Slice remaining banana; use to garnish gelatin. Place 1 cup in each treat box. Refrigerate until guests arrive.

To make ahead, refrigerate up to 24 hours. Garnish and serve as directed above.

1 serving contains:

Cal	Prot	Carb	Fat	Chol	Sodium
53	2g	11g	0	1mg	32mg

Makes 16 cookies.

**1/2 cup vegetable
shortening**

**2/3 cup lightly packed
brown sugar**

1 egg

1 teaspoon vanilla extract

1/2 teaspoon baking soda

**3/4 cup quick-cooking
rolled oats**

2 cups all-purpose flour

**1/3 cup smooth or
chunk-style peanut butter**

1/3 cup strawberry jam

In a mixer bowl, beat shortening and brown sugar until fluffy. Beat in egg, vanilla and baking soda. Stir in oats and flour; shape into 2 balls. Wrap each in plastic wrap or foil. Complete now or make ahead.

To complete now, refrigerate 1 hour. Preheat oven to 375F (190C). Roll out 1/2 of dough until 1/8-inch thick. Cut into 16 (3-inch) circles or cut with a jack-o'-lantern cutter. Spread each circle with 1 teaspoon peanut butter to within 1/2 inch of edge. Spread each with about 1 teaspoon jam. Roll out remaining dough 1/8 inch thick. Cut into 16 (3-inch) circles or cut with a jack-o'-lantern cutter. Cut a jack-o'-lantern face in each circle. Place cut-out circles on top of jam-covered circles. Press edges to seal. Place sandwiched cookies on an ungreased baking sheet. Bake 10 minutes or until lightly browned. Remove from baking sheet; cool on rack. Place 1 cookie in each treat box. Refrigerate until guests arrive. Serve cold.

To make ahead, refrigerate dough up to 2 hours; freeze up to 2 weeks. Thaw frozen dough in refrigerator overnight. To shape cookies, let dough stand at room temperature 15 minutes. Roll out, cut and bake cookies as directed above. Place cookies in a single layer in container with a tight-fitting lid. Refrigerate up to 3 days.

1 cookie contains:

Cal	Prot	Carb	Fat	Chol	Sodium
216	4g	29g	10g	13mg	60mg

Bewitching Gorp

Makes about 5 cups.

**1/2 cup shelled sunflower
seeds**

2 cups crispy rice cereal

1/4 cup shaved coconut

1/4 cup honey

2 tablespoons vegetable oil

1/2 teaspoon vanilla extract

1/2 cup golden raisins

**1-1/2 cups chopped mixed
dried fruit**

Preheat oven to 325F (165C). In a 13" x 9" baking
pan, combine seeds, cereal and coconut. In a
cup, combine honey, oil and vanilla. Stir into
cereal mixture. Bake 15 minutes, stirring
occasionally. Stir in dried fruit. Cool to room
temperature. Complete now or make ahead.

To complete now, spoon into 10 to 12 plastic
bags. Tie each with orange yarn or string. Place
1 bag in each treat box.

To make ahead, place in container with a
tight-fitting lid. Store at room temperature up to
7 days. Serve as directed above.

1 tablespoon contains:

Cal	Prot	Carb	Fat	Chol	Sodium
25	0	4g	1g	0	9mg

❖ *Double or triple the recipe and give these
packets to your trick-or-treaters.*

Thanksgiving

❖ *Menu* ❖

Golden-Grove Salad
Thanksgiving Roll-Ups
Stuffed Sweet Potatoes
Baked Sweet & Sour Onions
Persimmon-Nut Bread
Pumpkin-Pecan Cheesecake

Serves 8.

Timetable:

- Thanksgiving Roll-Ups – Freeze stuffed chicken breasts up to 1 month. Or make roll-ups and sauce up to 24 hours ahead.
- Persimmon-Nut Bread – Make up to 7 days ahead.
- Pumpkin-Pecan Cheesecake – Make up to 24 hours ahead.
- Baked Sweet & Sour Onions – Make up to 24 hours ahead. Bake just before serving.
- Stuffed Sweet Potatoes – Bake and stuff potatoes up to 24 hours ahead.
- Golden-Grove Salad – Section citrus and make dressing up to 24 hours ahead; refrigerate separately.

Shortcuts:

- Serve plain baked or mashed sweet potatoes.
- Use French-style salad dressing with Golden-Grove Salad.

Golden-Grove Salad *(Cover photo)*

Makes about 8 servings.

**2 tablespoons white-wine
vinegar**

1 teaspoon lemon juice

3 tablespoons sugar

1/2 teaspoon grated onion

1/4 teaspoon salt

1/4 teaspoon dry mustard

1/8 teaspoon paprika

1/3 cup vegetable oil

1 teaspoon celery seeds

Lettuce leaves

1 ripe avocado

**2 large oranges, peeled,
sectioned**

**2 medium grapefruit,
peeled, sectioned**

**2 to 3 tablespoons
pomegranate seeds**

In a blender or food processor, combine vinegar, lemon juice, sugar, onion, salt, dry mustard and paprika. With machine running, gradually pour in oil until well blended. Add celery seeds; set aside. Complete now or make ahead.

To complete now, arrange lettuce leaves in a platter. Peel and slice avocado. Arrange avocado slices alternately with orange and grapefruit sections. Sprinkle with pomegranate seeds. Spoon dressing over fruit or serve separately.

To make ahead, refrigerate orange and grapefruit segments and dressing separately up to 24 hours. Serve as directed above.

1 serving contains:

Cal	Prot	Carb	Fat	Chol	Sodium
175	1g	16g	13g	0	70mg

A time for families to gather together and enjoy traditional flavors served in new ways. Although you may not be ready to break completely with tradition, we hope you'll include several of these recipes.

Thanksgiving Roll-Ups

Makes 4 to 8 servings.

8 chicken-breast halves, boned, skinned

2 tablespoons butter or margarine

6 medium mushrooms, chopped

1/4 cup chopped pistachios

1/2 cup chopped cooked ham

1/2 cup soft breadcrumbs

1/2 teaspoon salt

1/8 teaspoon pepper

White-Wine Sauce:

2 teaspoons cornstarch

1/2 cup dry white wine

1/4 cup butter or margarine, melted

1/4 cup apricot preserves

1/4 cup fruit chutney, chopped

3 or 4 thin orange slices

Parsley sprig

Whole pistachios

Place chicken between 2 pieces of waxed paper and lightly pound to an even thickness; set aside. In a skillet, melt 2 tablespoons butter or margarine. Sauté mushrooms, chopped pistachios and ham. Stir in breadcrumbs. Sprinkle chicken with salt and pepper. Spoon stuffing in center of each breast; roll and secure with wooden picks. Complete now or make ahead.

To complete now, preheat oven to 350F (175C). Place rolls, seam-side down, in a 13" x 9" baking pan. Make White-Wine Sauce; spoon over roll-ups and bake 30 to 40 minutes. Baste during baking. To serve, top with remaining sauce. Garnish with orange slices, parsley sprig and pistachios.

To make White-Wine Sauce, in a saucepan, stir cornstarch and wine until smooth. Stir in butter or margarine, apricot preserves and chutney. Stirring constantly, cook until translucent.

To make ahead, place rolls, seam-side down, in a 13" x 9" baking pan. Cover and refrigerate up to 24 hours. Or place on a baking sheet. Freeze until firm. Wrap and freeze up to 1 month. Thaw overnight in refrigerator. Make sauce up to 24 hours ahead; refrigerate. Bake 40 to 50 minutes as directed above.

1 serving contains:

Cal	Prot	Carb	Fat	Chol	Sodium
297	31g	12g	13g	96mg	415mg

Stuffed Sweet Potatoes

Makes 8 servings.

4 large sweet potatoes or yams

1/2 lb. bulk pork sausage

1 cooking apple, peeled, cored, chopped

1/4 teaspoon ground cinnamon

1/2 teaspoon grated orange peel

2 tablespoons maple syrup

2 tablespoons butter, melted

1/4 cup chopped walnuts

Preheat oven to 400F (205C). Place potatoes in a 9-inch-square baking pan. Bake 50 to 60 minutes or until tender. Cut in half lengthwise. Scoop pulp into a bowl, leaving 1/4 inch of pulp in each shell. Mash pulp; set aside. In a skillet, sauté sausage. Drain fat. Add apple and sauté over medium heat until apple is tender and sausage is no longer pink; drain. Add sausage mixture to mashed sweet potatoes. Stir in cinnamon, orange peel and maple syrup. Spoon into sweet-potato shells. Grease a 13" x 9" baking pan; arrange stuffed shells in pan. Complete now or make ahead.

To complete now, reduce oven temperature to 350F (175C). Brush tops of stuffed potatoes with melted butter. Sprinkle walnuts on top. Bake 30 minutes. Place on a serving plate; serve hot.

To make ahead, cover and refrigerate up to 24 hours. Bake and serve as directed above.

1 serving contains:

Cal	Prot	Carb	Fat	Chol	Sodium
214	6g	21g	12g	26mg	324mg

Makes 8 servings.

2 bacon slices, diced

4 large onions, peeled, halved crosswise

2 tablespoons red-wine vinegar

2 tablespoons brown sugar

1/2 teaspoon Dijon-style mustard

1/2 teaspoon salt

1/8 teaspoon pepper

In a skillet, cook bacon until crisp. Remove bacon and set aside. Place onions, cut-side down in skillet with bacon drippings. Brown both sides. Place onions, cut-side up in an ungreased, 11" x 7" baking dish. Spoon pan drippings over onions. In a bowl, combine vinegar, brown sugar, mustard, salt and pepper; spoon over onions. Sprinkle onions with reserved bacon. Complete now or make ahead.

To complete now, preheat oven to 350F (175C). Bake 35 to 40 minutes or until onions are tender. Place in a serving dish; pour pan drippings over onions. Serve hot.

To make ahead, cover and refrigerate up to 24 hours. Bake uncovered at 350F (175C) 45 to 50 minutes or until onions are tender. Serve as directed above.

1 serving contains:

Cal	Prot	Carb	Fat	Chol	Sodium
35	1g	6g	1g	3mg	201mg

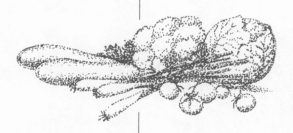

❖ *Incredibly tender with a refreshing combination of flavors.*

Persimmon-Nut Bread

Makes 1 (9" x 5") loaf.

2 ripe persimmons
1 tablespoon lemon juice
3/4 cup sugar
1/3 cup vegetable oil
2 eggs, lightly beaten
1/3 cup milk
1-3/4 cups all-purpose flour
1 teaspoon baking soda
1/2 teaspoon baking powder
1/2 teaspoon salt
1/2 teaspoon ground cinnamon
1/4 teaspoon ground cloves
1/2 cup chopped walnuts

Grease a 9" x 5" loaf pan. Preheat oven to 350F (175C). Cut persimmons crosswise; remove and discard seeds. Scoop out pulp. In a blender or food processor fitted with a metal blade, purée pulp and lemon juice. In a bowl, beat sugar, oil, eggs, milk and persimmon purée until combined. In a bowl, blend flour, baking soda, baking powder, salt, cinnamon, cloves and walnuts. Combine flour and persimmon mixtures. Spoon into greased pan. Bake 50 to 60 minutes or until a wooden pick inserted in center comes out clean. Turn onto a rack to cool. Complete now or make ahead.

To complete now, cool completely before slicing. To serve warm, reheat 15 minutes in a 350F (175C) oven.

To make ahead, bake up to 7 days ahead. Cool and wrap; refrigerate or freeze up to 7 days. Serve as directed above.

1 slice contains:

Cal	Prot	Carb	Fat	Chol	Sodium
236	4g	33g	10g	36mg	186mg

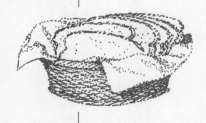

Pumpkin-Pecan Cheesecake

Makes 8 to 10 servings.

1-1/2 cups graham-cracker crumbs

1 tablespoon sugar

1/4 cup butter, melted

1/3 cup chopped pecans

2 (8-oz.) pkgs. Neufchâtel cheese

3/4 cup sugar

3 eggs

1/2 cup half and half

1 cup canned pumpkin

2 tablespoons maple syrup

1/2 teaspoon ground ginger

1/2 teaspoon ground cinnamon

1/4 teaspoon ground nutmeg

1 cup dairy sour cream

3 tablespoons sugar

1/4 teaspoon vanilla extract

1/3 cup pecan halves

In a bowl, combine graham-cracker crumbs, 1 tablespoon sugar, butter and chopped pecans. Press over bottom and 1-1/2 inches up side of an ungreased 9-inch springform pan; refrigerate. Preheat oven to 325F (165C). In a bowl, beat Neufchâtel cheese and 3/4 cup sugar until fluffy. Beat in eggs and half and half. Stir in pumpkin, maple syrup and spices. Pour into chilled crust. Bake 55 to 60 minutes. In a bowl, combine sour cream, 3 tablespoons sugar and vanilla. Spread over hot cheesecake. Arrange pecan halves over top. Bake 10 minutes. Let stand until cool. Complete now or make ahead.

To complete now, refrigerate at least 4 hours. To serve, remove side of pan and slice.

To make ahead, cover and refrigerate up to 4 days. Serve as directed above.

1 serving contains:

Cal	Prot	Carb	Fat	Chol	Sodium
470	10g	43g	30g	126mg	367mg

Happy Holiday

❖ *Menu* ❖

Holiday Appetizers
Star-of-Endive Salad
Regal-Crown Pork Roast
Orange-Spiced Figs
Green Beans Primo
Dinner Rolls
Frozen Lemon Cream

Serves 6 or 7.

Timetable:

- Holiday Appetizers – Make cheese mixture 2 to 3 days ahead.
- Frozen Lemon Cream – Make and freeze 2 to 3 days ahead.
- Orange-Spiced Figs – Make up to 24 hours ahead.
- Green Beans Primo – Make up to 24 hours ahead. Heat at serving time.
- Regal-Crown Pork Roast – Make stuffing up to 24 hours ahead. About 4 hours before serving, stuff and bake pork.
- Star-of-Endive Salad – Mix dressing and slice endive up to 12 hours ahead.

Shortcuts:

- Serve mixed green salad.
- Substitute spiced peaches for Orange-Spiced Figs.

Makes 32 appetizers.

1 (4-oz.) pkg. blue or Roquefort cheese

1/2 cup ricotta cheese

1/2 teaspoon Worcestershire sauce

2 teaspoons minced fresh chives or green onions

1/8 teaspoon salt

1/8 teaspoon pepper

1/2 teaspoon Dijon-style mustard

16 cherry tomatoes

Chopped green onion or chopped parsley

1 large zucchini

Pimiento strips

In a bowl or food processor, process blue or Roquefort cheese, ricotta cheese, Worcestershire sauce, chives or green onions, salt, pepper and mustard until blended. Complete now or make ahead.

To complete now, remove tops of cherry tomatoes. Scoop out centers. Invert tomato shells on paper towels 15 to 20 minutes. Spoon about 1-1/2 teaspoons cheese mixture into each drained tomato. Garnish tops with green onions or parsley. Cut zucchini into 16 crosswise slices; mound 1 teaspoon cheese mixture on each zucchini slice. Garnish with pimiento. Serve on a platter.

To make ahead, prepare cheese mixture 2 to 3 days ahead. Cover and refrigerate. About 3-1/2 hours before serving, prepare as directed above.

1 appetizer contains:

Cal	Prot	Carb	Fat	Chol	Sodium
20	1g	1g	1g	4mg	68mg

An elegant family dinner party. Delicious holiday fare plus sparkling Christmas decorations and candlelight accentuate the festive mood.

Star-of-Endive Salad

Makes 6 or 7 servings.

5 Belgian-endive heads

1/4 lb. medium mushrooms, sliced

1 tablespoon chopped pimiento

1/3 cup mayonnaise

1 teaspoon Dijon-style mustard

1 tablespoon minced chives

2 tablespoons minced watercress leaves

1/4 teaspoon salt

1/8 teaspoon pepper

1/4 teaspoon dried-leaf chervil, crushed

2 tablespoons olive oil or vegetable oil

2 tablespoons tarragon vinegar

1 tablespoon lemon juice

Remove 30 to 35 of largest outside endive leaves. Place large leaves in a plastic bag; refrigerate. Cut remaining endive into 1/4-inch crosswise slices. In a large bowl, combine sliced endive, mushrooms and pimiento. In a bowl, combine mayonnaise, mustard, chives, watercress, salt, pepper, chervil, oil, vinegar and lemon juice. Pour over mushroom mixture; toss to coat. Cover. Complete now or make ahead.

To complete now, refrigerate mushroom mixture 2 hours to let flavors blend. To serve, arrange 5 reserved leaves on each salad plate. Spoon salad mixture onto lined plates.

To make ahead, refrigerate up to 12 hours. Serve as directed above.

1 serving contains:

Cal	Prot	Carb	Fat	Chol	Sodium
91	1g	6g	8g	3mg	175mg

❖ *For added interest, arrange endive on clear glass salad plates in a star shape with the delicate tips pointed out.*

Regal-Crown Pork Roast

*Makes 6 or 7 servings
of 2 ribs each.*

1/2 cup golden raisins

**1/4 cup orange-flavored
liqueur**

3/4 lb. bulk pork sausage

1 small onion, chopped

**1 medium apple, peeled,
cored, diced**

1/2 cup chopped walnuts

**1/4 teaspoon ground
cinnamon**

**1/2 teaspoon grated orange
peel**

1/2 cup soft breadcrumbs

1 egg, lightly beaten

Salt and pepper

**1 (7- to 8-lb.) crown-rib
pork roast**

Kumquats

Maraschino cherries

In a bowl, combine raisins and liqueur; set aside. Crumble sausage into a skillet. Add onion; sauté until onion is soft and sausage is no longer pink. Drain fat. Stir in apple, walnuts, cinnamon, orange peel, breadcrumbs and reserved raisin mixture. Stir in egg. Complete now or make ahead.

To complete now, preheat oven to 325F (165C). Salt and pepper roast inside and outside; place on a broiler pan. Spoon stuffing into cavity of roast. Loosely cover stuffing and tips of bones with foil. Bake 3-1/2 to 4 hours or until meat thermometer inserted in thickest part of meat reaches 170F (75C). Place roast on a platter or serving plate. Place paper frills on tips of bones. Garnish with kumquats and maraschino cherries. To serve, spoon stuffing out of center; carve between ribs.

To make ahead, cover and refrigerate stuffing up to 24 hours. Stuff roast; bake, garnish and serve as directed above.

1 serving contains:

Cal	Prot	Carb	Fat	Chol	Sodium
491	40g	21g	25g	135mg	120mg

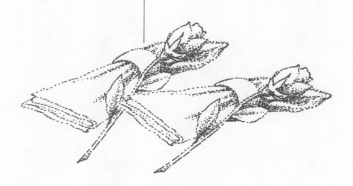

Orange-Spiced Figs

Makes 12 to 15 spiced figs.

1/2 cup sugar
1/2 cup red-wine vinegar
3/4 cup water
1 (3-inch) cinnamon stick
6 whole cloves
1 small orange, unpeeled
1 lb. fresh or dried figs
  (12 to 15), stemmed

In a saucepan, combine sugar, vinegar, water, cinnamon stick and cloves. Cut orange into 6 or 7 crosswise slices; cut each slice in half. Add to vinegar mixture. Bring to a boil; simmer 5 minutes. Place figs in a 1-1/2-quart heatproof bowl. Pour boiling syrup over figs. Cover. Let stand at room temperature about 30 minutes or if using dried figs, about 2 hours. Complete now or make ahead.

To complete now, drain; place figs around meat or in a serving bowl.

To make ahead, refrigerate figs in marinade up to 24 hours. Serve as directed above.

1 spiced fig contains:

Cal	Prot	Carb	Fat	Chol	Sodium
53	0	14g	0	0	1mg

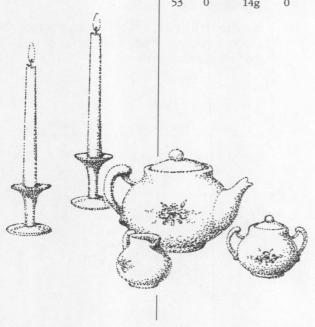

Green Beans Primo

Makes 6 to 8 servings.

**1 (20-oz.) pkg. frozen
French-style green beans
or 1-1/2 lbs. fresh green
beans, cut in julienne
strips**

2 tablespoons soy sauce

1 tablespoon vegetable oil

1 teaspoon sesame oil

1/4 cup sherry

1 garlic clove, crushed

1 teaspoon cornstarch

**1 (8-oz.) can whole water
chestnuts, drained, sliced**

Cook beans in lightly salted water 6 to 8 minutes
or until crisp-tender; drain. In a skillet, combine
soy sauce, vegetable oil, sesame oil, sherry and
garlic. Stir in cornstarch; stirring constantly, cook
until thickened. Gently stir in water chestnuts
and cooked beans until hot and coated with
sauce. Complete now or make ahead.

To complete now, spoon into a serving bowl;
serve hot.

To make ahead, cover and refrigerate 24 hours.
Reheat before serving.

1 serving contains:

Cal	Prot	Carb	Fat	Chol	Sodium
75	2g	11g	2g	0	265mg

❖ *Chestnuts supply a delightful crunchiness to
contrast tender green beans.*

Frozen Lemon Cream

Makes 6 to 8 servings.

3 eggs

1 cup sugar

1/2 teaspoon grated lemon peel

1/2 cup lemon juice

3/4 lb. soft chewy coconut macaroons

1 cup whipping cream

Whipping cream for garnish, if desired

Candied cherries, if desired

In a 1-1/2-quart saucepan, beat eggs and sugar until slightly thickened. Stir in lemon peel and juice. Stirring constantly, cook over very low heat until mixture thickens. Set aside to cool. Break macaroons into 1/2-inch pieces. Reserve 1 cup macaroon pieces. Line bottom and about 1 inch up side of an 8-inch springform pan with remaining macaroon pieces. Fold reserved macaroon pieces into cooled lemon mixture. Beat 1 cup whipping cream until soft peaks form; fold into lemon mixture. Carefully spoon into macaroon-lined pan. Complete now or make ahead.

To complete now, cover and freeze at least 4 hours or until firm. To serve, remove cover and side of pan. Cut frozen mixture into wedges. Garnish with whipped cream and cherry, if desired.

To make ahead, cover and freeze 2 to 3 days. Serve as directed above.

1 serving contains:

Cal	Prot	Carb	Fat	Chol	Sodium
373	4g	52g	17g	121mg	85mg

Bridal Shower

❖ Menu ❖

Honey-Roasted Nuts
Tarragon Eggs
International Canapés
Golden-State Chicken
Cinnamon-Apple Salad
Strawberry Ice-Cream Cake

Serves 10 to 12.

Timetable:

- International Canapés – Prepare and freeze up to 6 weeks.
- Honey-Roasted Nuts – Make up to 7 days ahead.
- Strawberry Ice-Cream Cake – Bake cake up to 7 days ahead; freeze. About 3 days before party, assemble and decorate cake.
- Golden-State Chicken – Bake up to 24 hours before party.
- Cinnamon-Apple Salad – Make and refrigerate up to 24 hours ahead.
- Tarragon Eggs – Cook eggs up to 24 hours ahead. Fill eggs 2 to 3 hours before serving.

Shortcuts:

- Purchase roasted nuts.
- Serve Strawberry Ice-Cream Cake and nuts and beverage.
- Omit 1 or 2 dishes.

Honey-Roasted Nuts

Makes about 2-1/2 cups.

2 tablespoons honey

1/4 teaspoon ground cinnamon

1/4 teaspoon ground mace

1 tablespoon butter or margarine, melted

1 (12-oz.) can mixed salted nuts

Preheat oven to 325F (165C). In a bowl, combine honey, cinnamon, mace and butter or margarine. Add mixed nuts; toss to coat. Spread in a 15" x 10" jelly-roll pan. Bake in preheated oven 10 minutes, stirring at least once. Cool to room temperature. Complete now or make ahead.

To complete now, serve in a decorative serving bowl.

To make ahead, store covered at room temperature up to 7 days. Serve as directed above.

1 tablespoon contains:

Cal	Prot	Carb	Fat	Chol	Sodium
58	1g	3g	5g	1mg	62mg

A light buffet to honor the radiant bride-to-be. The heart-shaped Strawberry Ice-Cream Cake crowns the sharing of best wishes and hope for the future.

Tarragon Eggs

Makes 24 appetizers.

12 hard-cooked eggs

**1/2 cup butter or
margarine, melted**

**1 cup diced cooked
chicken or turkey**

2 tablespoons half and half

**4 teaspoons chopped fresh
tarragon leaves**

2 teaspoons wine vinegar

1/2 teaspoon salt

1/4 teaspoon pepper

Tarragon leaves

Peel eggs; cut in half lengthwise. Remove egg yolks from whites; set egg whites aside. In a blender or food processor fitted with a metal blade, combine egg yolks, butter or margarine, chicken or turkey, half and half, chopped tarragon, vinegar, salt and pepper. Process until mixture is smooth. Complete now or make ahead.

To complete now, mound egg-yolk mixture into egg-white halves. Or spoon mixture into a pastry bag; pipe into egg-white halves. Garnish with tarragon leaves; arrange on a serving plate. Serve cold.

To make ahead, refrigerate cooked egg whites and egg-yolk mixture separately up to 24 hours. Assemble and serve as directed above.

1 appetizer contains:

Cal	Prot	Carb	Fat	Chol	Sodium
85	5g	0	7g	122mg	113mg

❖ *If fresh tarragon leaves are not available for garnish, use parsley, chives or watercress. Arrange on a plate lined with kale or butter lettuce leaves.*

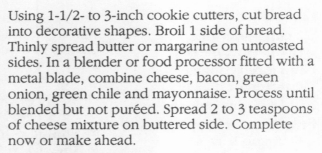

Makes 14 to 18 appetizers.

14 to 18 thin slices sandwich bread

1-1/2 to 2 tablespoons butter or margarine, room temperature

1 cup shredded Jarlsberg cheese (4 oz.)

2 bacon slices, cooked crisp, crumbled

1 green onion, chopped

1 fresh or canned green chile, chopped, or 2 tablespoons canned diced green chiles

1/4 cup mayonnaise

5 or 6 cherry tomatoes, each cut into 3 slices

Using 1-1/2- to 3-inch cookie cutters, cut bread into decorative shapes. Broil 1 side of bread. Thinly spread butter or margarine on untoasted sides. In a blender or food processor fitted with a metal blade, combine cheese, bacon, green onion, green chile and mayonnaise. Process until blended but not puréed. Spread 2 to 3 teaspoons of cheese mixture on buttered side. Complete now or make ahead.

To complete now, place canapés in a single layer on an ungreased baking sheet. Broil 5 to 6 inches from heat 2 to 4 minutes or until puffed and golden. Top each with cherry tomato slice. Arrange on a serving plate; serve warm.

To make ahead, freeze in a single layer on an ungreased baking sheet. When frozen, place in freezer bag. Freeze 1 to 6 weeks. Broil while frozen. Serve as directed above.

1 appetizer contains:

Cal	Prot	Carb	Fat	Chol	Sodium
95	4g	9g	5g	11mg	165mg

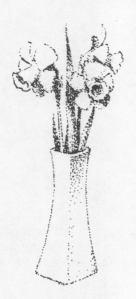

❖ *For a memorable table make a garland of fresh greens. Secure the greenery to a cord with fine wire, pin garland to edge of table cloth, accenting with ribbon and/or flowers.*

Golden-State Chicken

Makes 10 to 12 servings.

2 cups cubed, smoked, boneless chicken or turkey

1/4 cup toasted almonds

2 tablespoons chopped green onions

1/4 cup butter

1/4 cup all-purpose flour

1 cup milk

3 eggs, separated

1/2 cup chicken broth or bouillon

1/2 teaspoon dried-leaf tarragon, crushed

1/2 teaspoon salt

1/8 teaspoon pepper

1/2 teaspoon Dijon-style mustard

2 tablespoons white wine

About 36 asparagus spears, cooked

5 thin carrot slices

Grease a 9" x 5" loaf pan; set aside. In a food processor combine chicken or turkey, almonds and green onions. Process until finely chopped but not puréed; set aside. In a saucepan, melt butter; stir in flour. Stirring constantly, cook about 2 minutes. Stir in milk; continue stirring until smooth and thick; set aside. In a bowl, beat egg yolks until blended; stir in broth or bouillon. In a bowl, combine chicken or turkey and egg-yolk mixtures and sauce. Stir in dried tarragon, salt, pepper, mustard and wine. Beat egg whites until stiff but not dry; fold into combined mixture. Arrange 1/2 of asparagus crosswise in loaf pan, cutting stems to fit. Spoon 1/2 of chicken mixture over asparagus. Repeat layers with remaining chicken and asparagus. Complete now or make ahead.

To complete now, preheat oven to 350F (175C). Place loaf pan in a 13" x 9" baking pan; place both pans in preheated oven. Pour water about 1 inch deep in outer pan. Bake 55 to 65 minutes or until knife inserted in center comes out clean. Remove from hot water; let stand 5 minutes on a rack. Loosen edges from pan; invert onto a platter. Remove pan. Cut carrot slices into flower shapes; garnish top. Slice and serve warm. Or refrigerate until chilled and serve cold.

To make ahead, bake as directed above. Cover and refrigerate up to 24 hours. Reheat about 15 minutes in a 350F (175C) oven. Garnish and serve as directed above.

1 serving contains:

Cal	Prot	Carb	Fat	Chol	Sodium
161	12g	7g	10g	86mg	173mg

Makes 10 to 12 servings.

2/3 cup cold water

3 (1/4-oz.) envelopes unflavored gelatin

1-1/2 cups apple juice

1 cup red cinnamon candies

3 cups applesauce

1/2 cup plain lowfat yogurt

Lettuce leaves

1 (14-oz.) jar spiced crab apples, drained

Pour water into a 1-cup measuring cup. Sprinkle gelatin over water; set aside to soften, 3 minutes. Pour apple juice into a saucepan; add candies. Stir over medium heat until candies dissolve. Add softened gelatin; stir until dissolved. Remove from heat; stir in applesauce. Pour 1/2 of applesauce mixture into a 7- or 8-cup gelatin mold. Refrigerate in mold about 1-1/2 hours or until sticky on top. Reserve remaining applesauce mixture at room temperature. Stir yogurt into reserved applesauce mixture. Spoon over partially set gelatin. Cover. Complete now or make ahead.

To complete now, refrigerate 4 hours or until firm. Line a serving plate with lettuce leaves. Invert molded mixture onto lettuce-lined plate; remove mold. Garnish with spiced crab apples.

To make ahead, refrigerate up to 24 hours. Garnish and serve as directed above.

1 serving contains:

Cal	Prot	Carb	Fat	Chol	Sodium
111	2g	26g	0	1mg	15mg

Strawberry Ice-Cream Cake

Makes about 12 servings.

2 cups all-purpose flour

1-1/2 cups sugar

1/2 cup vegetable
shortening

1 cup milk

1 tablespoon baking
powder

1/2 teaspoon salt

1 teaspoon vanilla extract

4 eggs

1 qt. strawberry ice cream,
slightly softened

1 cup whipping cream

2 or 3 drops red food
coloring, if desired

1 tablespoon black-
raspberry liqueur,
if desired

1 pint strawberries

Grease and flour 2 (9-inch) heart-shape cake pans. Preheat oven to 350F (175C). In a mixer bowl, combine flour, sugar, shortening, milk, baking powder, salt and vanilla. Beat until blended. Increase to medium; beat about 30 seconds. Add eggs; beat 3 minutes. Spoon into prepared pans. Bake 25 to 30 minutes or until wooden pick inserted in center comes out clean. Cool in pan 5 minutes. Invert onto racks; remove pans. Cool. Complete now or make ahead.

To complete now, line bottom and side of cake pan with plastic wrap. Press ice cream into pan; freeze 4 hours. Place 1 cake layer, bottom-side up, on a serving plate. Invert ice cream onto cake layer; remove plastic wrap. Top with remaining cake layer; freeze 2 hours. Whip cream with food coloring and liqueur, if desired. Spread whipped cream thinly around side of cake. Return to freezer. Spoon remaining whipped cream into a pastry bag fitted with a star tip. Pipe a diagonal lattice design across top and a ruffle around top and bottom edges of cake. Freeze 2 to 3 hours or until firm. About 15 minutes before serving, cut strawberries in half; place in center of each lattice. Refrigerate no longer than 10 minutes. Serve chilled.

To make ahead, wrap and freeze cake layers up to 7 days. About 3 days before party, assemble and decorate cake as directed above. Freeze frosted cake. Garnish and serve as directed above.

1 serving contains:

Cal	Prot	Carb	Fat	Chol	Sodium
450	7g	55g	23g	120mg	249mg

Dynamic Dinner

❖ *Menu* ❖

Summer-Harvest Soup
Raspberry Chicken
Puréed Sweet Potatoes
Leeks Mimosa
Herbed Chèvre Bread
Peachy Almond Pizza

Serves 6 to 8.

Timetable:

- Summer-Harvest Soup – Make up to 24 hours ahead.
- Leeks Mimosa – Make up to 24 hours ahead; marinate overnight.
- Herbed Chèvre Bread – Make up to 24 hours ahead.
- Raspberry Chicken – Prepare chicken up to 24 hours ahead.
- Peachy Almond Pizza – Make crust and filling up to 24 hours ahead; refrigerate.

Shortcuts:

- Serve plain French bread.
- Use a pie-crust mix for crust of Peachy Almond Pizza.

Summer-Harvest Soup

Makes 5 or 6 servings.

4 bacon slices, chopped

1 small onion, chopped

4 yellow crookneck squash

2 cups fresh green peas or 1 (10-oz.) pkg. frozen green peas

2 cups chicken broth or bouillon

1/2 teaspoon salt

1/8 teaspoon pepper

1 teaspoon Worcestershire sauce

1/2 cup lowfat yogurt

1/2 teaspoon dried dill weed

Fresh dill sprigs

In a saucepan, cook bacon and onion until onion is soft. Dice unpeeled squash. Add diced squash, peas, broth or bouillon, salt, pepper and Worcestershire sauce to saucepan. Simmer until vegetables are tender, about 7 minutes. In a blender or food processor fitted with a metal blade, purée 1/2 of squash mixture at a time. Complete now or make ahead.

To complete now, return puréed mixture to saucepan; heat to boiling point. Remove from heat; stir in yogurt and dill weed. Serve in a soup tureen or in individual soup bowls. Garnish with dill sprigs.

To make ahead, cool, cover and refrigerate up to 24 hours. Reheat and serve as directed above.

1 serving contains:

Cal	Prot	Carb	Fat	Chol	Sodium
115	8g	12g	4g	10mg	392mg

Innovative touches added to these classic dishes reflect today's lighter cuisine. This beautiful presentation contrasts textures and flavors, creating a feast for the eye as well as the palate.

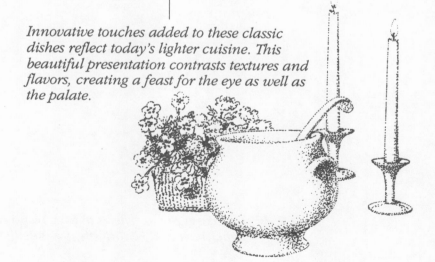

Raspberry Chicken (Cover photo)

Makes 8 servings.

8 chicken-breast halves

Salt and pepper to taste

2 tablespoons butter or margarine

2 tablespoons vegetable oil

1 (12-oz.) pkg. frozen unsweetened raspberries or 1 pint fresh raspberries

1/4 cup red wine

1 garlic clove, crushed

1 tablespoon minced parsley

1/2 cup chicken broth or bouillon

2 teaspoons green peppercorns, crushed

1/4 cup butter, cut in 1/2-inch pieces

Enoki mushrooms, if desired

Sprinkle chicken with salt and pepper. Heat 2 tablespoons butter or margarine and oil in a skillet. Add seasoned chicken; brown on both sides. Mash 1/2 of raspberries; press through a fine sieve to remove seeds. Refrigerate remaining berries. In a bowl, combine strained berries, wine, garlic, parsley and broth or bouillon. Pour over chicken. Cover skillet; cook 15 minutes. Complete now or make ahead.

To complete now, cook chicken in sauce until tender. Remove chicken and place on a serving dish; keep hot. Stir green peppercorns into sauce; remove from heat. Add 1/4 cup butter, 1 or 2 pieces at a time, stirring constantly until blended. Immediately spoon over chicken; garnish with reserved raspberries and enoki mushrooms, if desired. Serve hot.

To make ahead, refrigerate cooked chicken and sauce separately up to 24 hours. Reheat in a skillet, adding butter as directed above. Garnish and serve as directed above.

1 serving contains:

Cal	Prot	Carb	Fat	Chol	Sodium
287	28g	12g	14g	91mg	150mg

❖ *Our cover photo reflects today's trends of light, fresh and beautifully presented foods.*

Leeks Mimosa *(Cover photo)*

Makes 6 servings.

6 medium leeks, trimmed

2 cups beef broth or bouillon

1/3 cup tarragon vinegar

1 tablespoon chopped parsley

2 tablespoons sweet-pickle relish, drained

1 tablespoon chopped pimiento

1/2 teaspoon salt

1/4 teaspoon pepper

1/4 teaspoon paprika

1/2 cup vegetable oil or olive oil

Lettuce leaves

2 hard-cooked eggs, chopped

6 cherry tomatoes, halved

Cut off and discard green tops of leeks. Cut each leek in 4th's lengthwise. Wash thoroughly; drain on paper towels. Place leeks in a skillet. Add broth or bouillon. Cook covered 8 to 10 minutes or until tender. Drain and cool; place leeks in a shallow bowl. In a bowl, combine vinegar, parsley, relish, pimiento, salt, pepper, paprika and oil. Pour over leeks. Cover. Complete now or make ahead.

To complete now, refrigerate in marinade at least 2 hours. If olive oil is used, remove 30 minutes before serving. To serve, drain marinade. Arrange lettuce leaves on a serving dish; place leeks on top. Sprinkle with hard-cooked eggs. Garnish with cherry tomatoes; serve cold or at room temperature.

To make ahead, refrigerate in marinade up to 24 hours. Up to 3 hours before serving, drain marinade; arrange on lettuce leaves. Refrigerate until served. If olive oil is used, remove from refrigerator 30 minutes before serving. Garnish and serve as directed above.

1 serving contains:

Cal	Prot	Carb	Fat	Chol	Sodium
269	5g	19g	21g	71mg	258mg

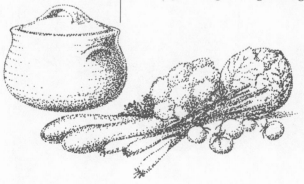

63

Herbed Chèvre Bread

Makes 6 to 8 servings.

1 (8-oz.) unsliced baguette French bread

4 to 5 oz. (chèvre) goat cheese, room temperature, cut in 1/2-inch pieces

1/2 cup butter or margarine, room temperature

1 teaspoon minced chives

1 tablespoon minced parsley

1/2 teaspoon Dijon-style mustard

1/4 teaspoon dried-leaf thyme or 3/4 teaspoon chopped thyme leaves

1/4 teaspoon dried dill weed or 1 teaspoon chopped fresh dill

Cut bread in half lengthwise. Cut each half in 1-inch crosswise slices, almost to bottom crust. Set aside. In a food processor fitted with a metal blade or a mixer, combine remaining ingredients. Keeping slices together, spread cheese mixture over cut side of each half of bread. Wrap each in foil. Complete now or make ahead.

To complete now, preheat oven to 400F (205C). Bake foil-wrapped bread 10 minutes or until hot. Cut slices apart; arrange in a serving bowl.

To make ahead, refrigerate up to 24 hours. Bake and serve as directed above.

1 serving contains:

Cal	Prot	Carb	Fat	Chol	Sodium
221	5g	15g	16g	44mg	423mg

Makes 6 to 8 servings.

1/4 cup brown sugar

3/4 cup all-purpose flour

1/4 cup butter or
  margarine, room
  temperature

1/4 cup finely chopped
  toasted almonds

1 (8-oz.) pkg. cream cheese

1/4 cup granulated sugar

1 egg

2 tablespoons lemon juice,
  divided

2 tablespoons milk

1/2 teaspoon vanilla extract

About 6 large ripe peaches

Peach Glaze:

1/2 cup sugar

2 tablespoons cornstarch

3/4 cup water

1 tablespoon almond-
  flavored liqueur

1 or 2 drops red food
  coloring

2 tablespoons toasted
  slivered almonds

Preheat oven to 400F (205C). In a bowl, combine brown sugar and flour. Cut in butter or margarine until crumbly. Stir in almonds. Press over bottom of a 12-inch pizza pan. Bake 10 to 12 minutes or until golden brown. Set aside. Beat cream cheese and granulated sugar until smooth. Beat in egg, 1 tablespoon lemon juice, milk and vanilla. Reduce heat to 350F (175C). Pour cheese mixture over baked crust. Return to oven; bake 20 to 25 minutes or until firm. Cool completely. Complete now or make ahead.

To complete now, peel and slice peaches; sprinkle with 1 tablespoon lemon juice. Remove 1 cup slices; mash with fork or purée in food processor. Arrange remaining peach slices over baked cheese mixture in spiral. Make Glaze, spoon over peaches. Top with almonds. Refrigerate 2 hours. To serve, cut into wedges.

To make Glaze, in a saucepan, combine sugar and cornstarch; stir in water and puréed peaches. Stirring constantly, cook over medium heat until mixture thickens. Press through strainer; stir in liqueur and food coloring.

To make ahead, cover cooled pizza crust; refrigerate up to 24 hours. Top with peach slices and glaze as directed above.

1 serving contains:

Cal	Prot	Carb	Fat	Chol	Sodium
360	5g	46g	18g	73mg	146mg

Summertime Brunch

❖ *Menu* ❖

Fennel Salad
Zucchini-Cheese Wheel
Broiled Tomatoes
Jumbo Popovers
Fresh Plum Butter
Chocolate-Flecked Logs
Fresh-Fruit Platter

Serves 6.

Timetable:

- Chocolate-Flecked Logs – Make and freeze up to 1 month.
- Jumbo Popovers – Make and freeze up to 7 days. Or refrigerate in custard cups 1 hour before baking.
- Zucchini-Cheese Wheel – Make and freeze up to 5 days. Or refrigerate up to 24 hours.
- Fresh Plum Butter – Make and refrigerate up to 4 days.
- Fennel Salad – Make up to 24 hours ahead.
- Broiled Tomatoes – Make up to 24 hours ahead.
- Fresh-Fruit Platter – Prepare fruit 3 or 4 hours ahead; cover and refrigerate.

Shortcuts:

- Purchase jam.
- Purchase muffins or a coffeecake.

Fennel Salad

Makes about 6 servings.

3 cups thinly sliced fennel

1 small red onion, thinly sliced

3 tablespoons red-wine vinegar

1 tablespoon lemon juice

1 teaspoon Dijon-style mustard

1/2 teaspoon salt

1/4 teaspoon pepper

2 tablespoons minced watercress leaves

1/2 cup olive oil or vegetable oil

Lettuce

1 tablespoon chopped pimiento

In a bowl, combine fennel and onion. In a cup, combine vinegar, lemon juice, mustard, salt, pepper, watercress and oil. Pour over fennel mixture; toss lightly. Cover. Complete now or make ahead.

To complete now, refrigerate at least 2 hours. To serve, drain vegetables. Spoon vegetables into lettuce-lined dish. Sprinkle with pimiento; serve cold.

To make ahead, refrigerate up to 24 hours. Serve as directed above.

1 serving contains:

Cal	Prot	Carb	Fat	Chol	Sodium
178	1g	4g	18g	0	202mg

Enjoy a casual warm-weather brunch on your patio or porch. Offer guests sparkling Mimosas or chilled fruit juice to sip. Piping hot Jumbo Popovers are teamed with Fresh Plum Butter.

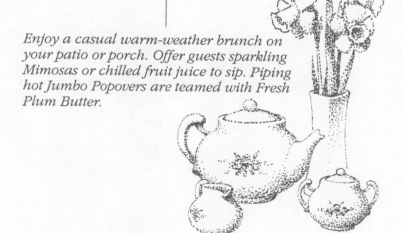

Zucchini-Cheese Wheel

Makes about 6 servings.

3 medium zucchini

2 tablespoons vegetable oil

2 eggs

1 cup cottage cheese

1/4 cup butter or margarine, room temperature

1/4 cup all-purpose flour

1/2 teaspoon baking powder

1/4 teaspoon salt

1 cup dairy sour cream

1 tablespoon minced green onion

3 slices boiled or baked ham, finely chopped (about 2 oz.)

1/4 cup grated Parmesan cheese (3/4 oz.)

Cut each zucchini into 6 lengthwise slices. Heat oil in a skillet; add zucchini slices. Cook over medium heat only until softened. Line bottom of an ungreased 8-inch springform pan with 6 slices cooked zucchini. Line side with remaining slices, letting ends drape over outside of pan; set aside. In a bowl, beat eggs. Beat in cottage cheese and butter or margarine until almost smooth. In a bowl, blend flour, baking powder and salt. Stir into egg mixture. Stir in sour cream, green onion, ham and Parmesan cheese. Spoon into zucchini-lined pan. Fold zucchini ends over filling toward center of pan. Complete now or make ahead.

To complete now, preheat oven to 350F (175C). Bake 40 to 50 minutes; cool on a wire rack 10 minutes. Remove side of springform pan. Cut wheel into wedges; serve warm or cold. To keep warm, cover; place on a hot tray.

To make ahead, cover; refrigerate up to 24 hours or freeze up to 5 days. Bake early enough before brunch to leave at least 1 hour to bake popovers. To bake refrigerated version, preheat oven to 350F (175C). Bake uncovered 40 to 50 minutes or until lightly browned. If frozen, thaw at room temperature 30 minutes; then bake, uncovered, in preheated oven 45 to 55 minutes until lightly browned. Serve as directed above.

1 serving contains:

Cal	Prot	Carb	Fat	Chol	Sodium
298	13g	8g	24g	118mg	565mg

Broiled Tomatoes

Makes 6 servings.

3 medium tomatoes
1/2 cup soft breadcrumbs
1/2 teaspoon dried-leaf basil
1/4 teaspoon salt
1/8 teaspoon pepper
1 tablespoon butter

Cut tomatoes in half crosswise. Make 4 or 5 (1/4-inch-deep) slashes across cut-side of each tomato half. In a bowl, combine breadcrumbs, basil, salt and pepper. Sprinkle on cut-side of each tomato half. Dot each with butter. Complete now or make ahead.

To complete now, broil crumb-topped tomatoes, 5 to 6 inches from heat, until golden brown. Arrange on a serving dish; serve hot.

To make ahead, cover; refrigerate up to 24 hours. Remove cover; broil and serve as directed.

1 serving contains:

Cal	Prot	Carb	Fat	Chol	Sodium
40	1g	5g	2g	5mg	130mg

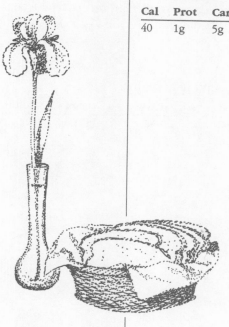

Jumbo Popovers

Makes 6 servings.

3 eggs
1 cup milk
2 tablespoons butter or
margarine, melted
1 cup all-purpose flour
1/4 teaspoon salt

Generously grease 6 (6-ounce) custard cups; set aside. In a bowl or blender, beat all ingredients until smooth. Pour into greased cups. Complete now or make ahead.

To complete now, preheat oven to 400F (205C). Place filled custard cups in a jelly-roll pan. Bake in preheated oven 40 to 50 minutes or until browned and center is moist but not gummy. Cut open 1 popover to test for doneness. Serve hot.

To make ahead, refrigerate batter in custard cups up to 1 hour. Place cups in a jelly-roll pan. Bake in preheated oven 50 to 60 minutes or until browned and center is moist but not gummy; serve hot. If desired, freeze baked popovers up to 7 days. To reheat, return to custard cups. Preheat oven to 350F (175C); heat 8 to 10 minutes.

1 serving contains:

Cal	Prot	Carb	Fat	Chol	Sodium
167	7g	18g	7g	121mg	172mg

❖ *Impress everyone with these truly delicious beauties. Once you see how easy they are to do, you'll make them often.*

Fresh Plum Butter

Makes 2-1/2 to 3 cups.

**4 ripe plums, pitted,
chopped**
1 cup powdered sugar
**1 cup butter, room
temperature**

In a blender or food processor fitted with a metal blade, combine plums, powdered sugar and butter. Blend until smooth and creamy. Complete now or make ahead.

To complete now, spoon into serving dish; refrigerate at least 15 minutes. Serve slightly chilled. Use leftovers on toast or muffins the next day.

To make ahead, refrigerate up to 4 days.

1 tablespoon contains:

Cal	Prot	Carb	Fat	Chol	Sodium
45	0	3g	4g	10mg	32mg

Chocolate-Flecked Logs

Makes about 20 logs.

1/4 cup butter
1/2 cup granulated sugar
2 teaspoons grated orange peel
1 oz. semi-sweet chocolate, grated
2 egg whites
1/2 cup all-purpose flour
Powdered sugar

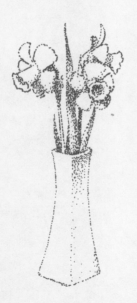

Preheat oven to 325F (165C). In a bowl, beat butter and granulated sugar until fluffy. Stir in orange peel and chocolate. In a bowl, beat egg whites until stiff but not dry. Fold into chocolate mixture alternately with flour. Drop by heaping teaspoons about 3 inches apart on an ungreased baking sheet. Dip the back of a spoon in water and flatten each mound into a 3-inch circle. Bake 10 minutes. Working quickly, roll warm cookie around handle of a wooden spoon. Gently remove from handle. If cookies becomes too stiff to roll, return to oven for a few minutes. Cool, seam-side down, on a wire rack. Complete now or make ahead.

To complete now, sprinkle cooled logs with powdered sugar; arrange on a serving plate. Serve immediately.

To make ahead, freeze covered up to 1 month. Thaw at room temperature. Serve as directed above.

1 log contains:

Cal	Prot	Carb	Fat	Chol	Sodium
60	1g	8g	3g	6mg	25mg

Tailgate Party

❖ Menu ❖

Golden-Harvest Soup
Buttered French Bread
Sportsmen's Special
Mixed Green Salad
Orange-Apricot Bars
Fresh Fruit

Serves 6.

Timetable:

- Orange-Apricot Bars – Make and freeze up to 2 months.
- Golden-Harvest Soup – Make up to 24 hours ahead.
- Sportsmen's Special – Make up to 24 hours ahead.

Shortcuts:

- Serve Melba toast instead of French bread.
- Purchase cookies.

Golden-Harvest Soup

Makes about 8 servings.

2 lbs. banana or hubbard squash or 2 (10-oz.) pkgs. frozen squash

2 cups dairy sour cream

2 cooking apples, peeled, cored, cubed

1/2 teaspoon ground nutmeg

Salt and pepper to taste

2 tablespoons chopped onion

1/4 cup butter or margarine

1/4 cup all-purpose flour

4 cups chicken broth or bouillon

4 bacon slices, cooked crisp, crumbled

Place squash, skin-side down, in a 13" x 9" baking pan; cover with foil. Place pan in oven. Bake at 425F (220C) 60 minutes or until tender. Peel and cut pulp into 1-inch cubes. In a blender or food processor, process sour cream, apples, nutmeg, salt, pepper, onion and 1/2 of squash until smooth. Pour into a bowl; purée remaining squash. In a skillet, melt butter or margarine. Stir in flour; stirring constantly, cook about 2 minutes. Gradually stir in broth or bouillon. Cook, stirring, until sauce is slightly thickened. Stir in purée. Complete now or make ahead.

To complete now, heat, do not boil. Pour into a thermos for transporting. Serve in soup bowls or mugs; sprinkle with bacon.

To make ahead, cover and refrigerate up to 24 hours. Reheat. Serve as directed above.

1 serving contains:

Cal	Prot	Carb	Fat	Chol	Sodium
310	9g	23g	22g	48mg	207mg

Welcome Fall with a tailgate party. You don't need a station wagon; take a folding table and chairs. Sit back, relax and enjoy our portable meal.

Makes 6 servings.

2 tablespoons vegetable oil

3 medium zucchini, sliced

1 medium onion, sliced

1 lb. lean ground beef

1/2 lb. mild Italian sausage

1/4 teaspoon dried-leaf oregano

1 garlic clove, crushed

1/8 teaspoon ground cloves

Salt and pepper to taste

1 (6-oz.) can tomato paste

1/2 cup dry red wine

1/3 cup butter or margarine

1/3 cup all-purpose flour

2 cups half and half

1 cup chicken broth or bouillon

1/4 teaspoon salt

1/8 teaspoon ground nutmeg

1/4 cup grated Parmesan cheese (3/4 oz.)

Heat oil in a skillet. Sauté zucchini and onion. Drain on paper towels. In same skillet, brown ground beef and sausage; discard drippings. Stir in oregano, garlic, cloves, salt and pepper to taste, tomato paste and wine. Simmer 5 minutes; remove from heat. In a heavy saucepan, melt butter or margarine. Stir in flour; stirring, cook 2 minutes. Stir in half and half, broth or bouillon, 1/4 teaspoon salt and nutmeg. Cook over medium heat, stirring, until mixture thickens; remove from heat. Spread drained zucchini and onion evenly in an ungreased 13" x 9" baking dish. Sprinkle with cheese. Spread meat mixture over cheese; then top with sauce. Complete now or make ahead.

To complete now, bake at 350F (175C) 35 to 45 minutes or until bubbly. To transport, immediately cover tightly with foil. Wrap completely with 5 or 6 layers of newspaper to keep hot. To serve, spoon onto individual plates.

To make ahead, cover with foil; refrigerate up to 24 hours. Bake uncovered in 350F (175C) oven 45 to 55 minutes. Transport and serve as directed above.

1 serving contains:

Cal	Prot	Carb	Fat	Chol	Sodium
506	25g	18g	36g	114mg	541mg

❖ *This is a pleasant change from usual cold sandwich fare.*

Orange-Apricot Bars

Makes 32 to 40 bars.

2 cups chopped dried
    apricots

1 orange, peeled, seeded,
    chopped

1-1/2 cups water

1/2 cup granulated sugar

1/2 cup chopped blanched
    almonds, toasted

2 cups all-purpose flour

2 cups quick-cooking
    rolled oats

3/4 cup lightly packed
    brown sugar

1 cup butter or margarine

1 tablespoon butter or
    margarine, melted

1 cup powdered sugar

1 to 1-1/2 tablespoons
    lemon juice or orange
    juice

In a saucepan, combine apricots, orange, water and granulated sugar. Stirring, simmer 15 minutes or until thickened. Stir in almonds; set aside. Preheat oven to 375F (190C). Grease a 13" x 9" baking pan. In a bowl, combine flour, rolled oats and brown sugar. Cut in 1 cup butter or margarine with a pastry blender or 2 knives until mixture resembles coarse crumbs. Pat 1/2 of oat mixture over bottom of greased pan. Spread apricot mixture over crumbs. Top with remaining 1/2 of crumbs; pat gently. Bake 30 minutes. Cool in pan. In a bowl, combine 1 tablespoon butter or margarine, powdered sugar and enough juice to make a smooth glaze. Drizzle over cooled mixture. After glaze sets, cut into bars. Complete now or make ahead.

To complete now, place glazed bars in container with lid for transporting.

To make ahead, store glazed bars covered at room temperature up to 24 hours. Or wrap in freezer wrap; freeze up to 2 months. Thaw at room temperature.

1 bar contains:

Cal	Prot	Carb	Fat	Chol	Sodium
142	2g	21g	6g	13mg	44mg

School Reunion

❖ *Menu* ❖

Honey-Roasted Nuts, page 54
Vegetable Starters
Oriental Meatballs
Monsoon Pork Satay
Spiced Zucchini Sticks, page 19
Mini Almond Cakes
Chocolate-Hazelnut Cookies

Serves 20 to 25.

Timetable:

- Mini Almond Cakes – Make and freeze up to 1 month. Or store up to 7 days.
- Chocolate-Hazelnut Cookies – Bake and freeze up to 1 month. Or bake up to 24 hours ahead.
- Oriental Meatballs – Make and freeze meatballs up to 3 weeks. Or make up to 24 hours ahead; refrigerate.
- Honey-Roasted Nuts – Make up to 7 days ahead.
- Spiced Zucchini Sticks – Make up to 7 days ahead.
- Monsoon Pork Satay – Make up to 24 hours ahead.
- Vegetable Starters – Make up to 2 hours ahead.

Shortcuts:

- Purchase mixed nuts.
- Purchase cookies.
- Steam zucchini, omit spices.

Vegetable Starters

Makes about 16 turnip and 46 jícama appetizers.

2 medium turnips

1 jícama (about 2 lbs.)

2 cups shredded sharp cheddar cheese (8 oz.)

1/4 cup reduced-calorie mayonnaise

1 teaspoon Dijon-style mustard

1/8 teaspoon paprika

1/2 teaspoon Worcestershire sauce

1/4 teaspoon salt

Pimiento-stuffed green olives, sliced

Watercress

Pimiento strips

Cut turnips and jícama crosswise into 1/4-inch slices. Cut designs using 1-1/2 to 2-inch cookie cutters. In a food processor, process cheese, mayonnaise, mustard, paprika, Worcestershire sauce and salt until blended. Spoon into pastry bag fitted with large star tip. Pipe a swirl of cheese mixture onto each cutout. Top with an olive slice, watercress sprig or pimiento strip. Complete now or make ahead.

To complete now, arrange on a platter.

To make ahead, refrigerate covered up to 2 hours.

1 turnip appetizer contains:

Cal	Prot	Carb	Fat	Chol	Sodium
24	1g	1g	2g	5mg	55mg

1 jícama appetizer contains:

Cal	Prot	Carb	Fat	Chol	Sodium
23	1g	2g	1g	4mg	36mg

An eye-catching array of tasty finger foods is sure to please your friends. Vegetable hearts, flowers, stars or bells add a festive touch to your appetizer tray.

Oriental Meatballs

Makes 36 meatballs and 1-1/4 cups sauce.

1/2 lb. uncooked shrimp, shelled, deveined, chopped

1/2 lb. uncooked lean pork, chopped

1/2 cup chopped celery stalks and leaves

1/4 cup chopped green onions

1 (8-oz.) can water chestnuts, drained

2 eggs, lightly beaten

1 tablespoon soy sauce

1/4 cup soft breadcrumbs

1/2 teaspoon salt

1/4 teaspoon pepper

Dipping Sauce:

1/2 cup plain yogurt

1/2 cup fruit chutney, finely chopped

1/2 teaspoon curry powder

1/4 cup dry white wine

1/4 teaspoon grated ginger root

Preheat oven to 375F (190C). In a food processor combine shrimp, pork, celery, green onions and water chestnuts. Process until finely chopped. In a bowl, combine eggs, soy sauce, breadcrumbs, salt, pepper and meat mixture. Shape into 36 (1-inch) balls. Arrange on a broiler pan. Bake 18 to 20 minutes or until golden brown. Drain; discard drippings. Complete now or make ahead.

To complete now, prepare Dipping Sauce. Keep meatballs warm in a chafing dish or on a hot tray. Serve with Dipping Sauce.

To make Dipping Sauce, in a bowl, combine all sauce ingredients.

To make ahead, cover and refrigerate cooked meatballs up to 24 hours. Freeze up to 3 weeks. Make and refrigerate Dipping Sauce up to 24 hours ahead. Thaw meatballs in refrigerator overnight. To reheat, arrange meatballs in a pan; cover with foil. Heat at 350F (175C) 15 minutes or until warm. Serve as directed above.

1 meatball contains:

Cal	Prot	Carb	Fat	Chol	Sodium
23	3g	1g	1g	28mg	83mg

1 tablespoon sauce contains:

Cal	Prot	Carb	Fat	Chol	Sodium
10	0	2g	0	0	5mg

Makes about 60 meat cubes or about 20 appetizer servings.

1/4 cup soy sauce

1/4 cup dry white wine

2 tablespoons brown sugar

1 garlic clove, crushed

1/2 cup vegetable oil

1 lb. boneless pork or boneless chicken breast, cut in 1-inch cubes

Dipping Sauce:

1/4 cup chunk-style peanut butter

1/2 teaspoon crushed dried red-pepper flakes

1 teaspoon grated fresh ginger

2 tablespoons honey

1 tablespoon lemon juice

1 green onion, chopped

2 tablespoons dry white wine

In a bowl, combine soy sauce, wine, brown sugar, garlic and oil. Add pork or chicken; spoon marinade over meat. Cover. Complete now or make ahead.

To complete now, marinate meat in refrigerator at least 4 hours. Prepare Dipping Sauce. Drain meat and discard marinade. Place meat cubes on a broiler pan. Broil meat about 6 inches from heat until all sides are browned. Arrange broiled meat on a serving plate. Insert a wooden pick into each meat cube. Serve with sauce.

To make Dipping Sauce, in a blender or food processor fitted with a metal blade, combine all sauce ingredients. Process until almost smooth.

To make ahead, refrigerate meat in marinade up to 24 hours. Make and refrigerate Dipping Sauce up to 24 hours ahead. Broil and serve as directed above.

1 serving contains:

Cal	Prot	Carb	Fat	Chol	Sodium
109	6g	4g	7g	13mg	237mg

❖ *Try this zesty marinade on shrimp. Marinate about 1 hour before broiling.*

Mini Almond Cakes

Makes about 60 mini-cakes.

1/2 teaspoon baking powder

1/2 cup all-purpose flour

1/2 cup butter, room temperature

1 (7- or 8-oz.) pkg. almond paste, room temperature

3/4 cup sugar

3 eggs

1 teaspoon grated orange peel

2/3 cup sliced almonds

Place paper bon-bon cups in about 60 (1-3/4-inch) muffin cups. Preheat oven to 350F (175C). In a bowl, combine baking powder and flour; set aside. In a bowl, beat butter and almond paste until creamy. Add sugar; beat until light and fluffy. Add eggs, 1 at a time, beating well after each addition. Beat reserved flour mixture into egg mixture until smooth; stir in orange peel. Spoon about 1 teaspoon mixture into each bon-bon cup. Sprinkle with almonds. Bake 15 to 20 minutes or until golden brown. Complete now or make ahead.

To complete now, cool about 5 minutes on a rack. Remove from muffin pans; arrange on a serving plate. Serve warm or cool to room temperature before serving.

To make ahead, cool and remove from muffin cups. Store covered up to 1 week at room temperature. Or arrange in a single layer on baking sheets; freeze. Place in freezer bags and store frozen up to 1 month. Thaw at room temperature at least 1 hour before serving.

1 mini-cake contains:

Cal	Prot	Carb	Fat	Chol	Sodium
52	1g	5g	3g	15mg	19mg

Chocolate-Hazelnut Cookies

Makes about 40 cookies.

1/3 cup ground blanched hazelnuts

1 tablespoon unsweetened cocoa powder

1/4 cup cornstarch

1/4 cup sugar

3 egg whites, room temperature

1/8 teaspoon cream of tartar

1/2 teaspoon vanilla extract

1/3 cup sugar

Grease a baking sheet; set aside. Preheat oven to 325F (165C). In a bowl, combine ground hazelnuts, cocoa powder, cornstarch and 1/4 cup sugar; set aside. In a bowl, beat egg whites, cream of tartar and vanilla until foamy. Gradually beat in 1/3 cup sugar until stiff peaks form. Fold cocoa mixture into beaten egg whites. Drop by teaspoons about 1 inch apart on baking sheet, making a curl on top with back of spoon. Bake 20 to 25 minutes or until tips begin to brown. Let stand 5 minutes. Remove from baking sheet; cool completely on a wire rack. Complete now or make ahead.

To complete now, arrange cooled cookies on a serving plate. Serve immediately.

To make ahead, place cooled cookies in a single layer in container with a tight-fitting lid. Store up to 1 week. Or freeze up to 1 month. Serve as directed above.

1 cookie contains:

Cal	Prot	Carb	Fat	Chol	Sodium
21	0	4g	1g	0	4mg

Winter Supper

❖ *Menu* ❖

Mixed Nuts
Popcorn
Hot Buttered Cider
Hearty Three-Bean Stew
Dilly Cheese Slices
Orange Sponge Cake

Serves 6 to 8.

Timetable:

- Orange Sponge Cake – Make and freeze up to 2 months.
- Dilly Cheese Slices – Make and freeze up to 7 days.
- Hot Buttered Cider – Make 3 or 4 days ahead.
- Hearty Three-Bean Stew – Make up to 24 hours ahead.

Shortcuts:

- Substitute peanuts for mixed nuts
- Purchase a similar cake.
- Purchase a loaf of bread.

Hot Buttered Cider

Makes 6 to 8 servings.

6 cups apple cider

**1/4 teaspoon ground
nutmeg**

**1/8 teaspoon ground
cardamom**

2 (3-inch) cinnamon sticks

1/3 cup rum

4 teaspoons butter

In a 2-quart saucepan, combine cider, nutmeg, cardamom and cinnamon. Bring to a boil. Cover; simmer 5 minutes. Set aside to cool. Complete now or make ahead.

To complete now, remove cinnamon sticks; heat to boiling. Remove from heat; stir in rum. Pour into mugs. Top each with about 1/2 teaspoon butter; serve immediately.

To make ahead, cover; refrigerate up to 4 days. Reheat before serving as directed above.

1 serving contains:

Cal	Prot	Carb	Fat	Chol	Sodium
122	0	21g	2g	5mg	29mg

*After a cold day, enjoy hot and hearty food.
For a homey touch, scoop out a round loaf of
French bread and use it as a serving bowl
for Hearty Three-Bean Stew.*

Hearty Three-Bean Stew

Makes 8 servings.

1 lb. beef shank

1 lb. ham hock

1 medium onion, chopped

1 carrot, finely chopped

**2 medium tomatoes,
  peeled, seeded, chopped**

1 garlic clove, crushed

**1/4 teaspoon dried-leaf
  thyme**

1 teaspoon salt

1/4 teaspoon pepper

**1 (15-oz.) can kidney
  beans, drained**

**1 (15-oz.) can garbanzo
  beans, drained**

**1 (15-oz.) can lima beans,
  drained**

**1/2 lb. smoked sausage,
  thinly sliced**

In a 4- or 6-quart saucepan, combine beef shank, ham hock, onion, carrot, tomatoes, 6 cups water, garlic, thyme, salt and pepper. Bring to a boil. Cover; gently cook 1-1/2 hours or until meat is very tender. Remove beef shank and ham hock; reserve ingredients in saucepan. Cut meat from bones; discard bones. Return meat to pan. Complete now or make ahead.

To complete now, add beans and sausage. Cover; simmer 15 minutes. Serve hot.

To make ahead, let stew cool. Cover; refrigerate up to 24 hours. To serve, pour into saucepan; add beans and sausage. Cover; simmer 15 minutes. Or heat in slow cooker 3 to 4 hours, adding beans and sausage last 30 minutes.

1 serving contains:

Cal	Prot	Carb	Fat	Chol	Sodium
323	20g	37g	11g	34mg	896mg

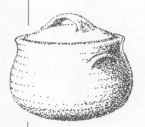

❖ *Surprise your guests with this combination of flavorful meats and colorful beans.*

Dilly Cheese Slices

Makes 14 to 16 slices.

1 (16-oz.) loaf French bread, unsliced

1/4 cup butter

5 cups shredded cheddar cheese (1-1/4 lbs.)

2 teaspoons dried dill weed

1/8 teaspoon pepper

2 teaspoons Worcestershire sauce

1 teaspoon grated onion

3 eggs, lightly beaten

Cut bread crosswise into 1-inch slices. Cut crust from slices; use for another purpose. In a saucepan, combine butter and cheese. Stir over low heat until both are melted. Stir in dill weed, pepper, Worcestershire sauce and onion. Stirring constantly, add eggs; beat or whisk until well blended. Remove from heat. Dip bread slices into hot mixture, turning to coat both sides. Shake off excess sauce. Place coated slices on 2 ungreased baking sheets. Complete now or make ahead.

To complete now, preheat oven to 350F (175C). Bake coated slices 15 to 18 minutes or until hot and bubbly. Serve warm.

To make ahead, freeze coated slices on baking sheets about 2 hours. When frozen, individually wrap each slice. Place in freezer bag; store in freezer up to 7 days. About 30 minutes before serving time, preheat oven to 350F (175C). Unwrap slices; place on baking sheets in a single layer. Bake frozen slices 20 to 22 minutes or until hot and bubbly.

1 slice contains:

Cal	Prot	Carb	Fat	Chol	Sodium
264	13g	15g	17g	85mg	448mg

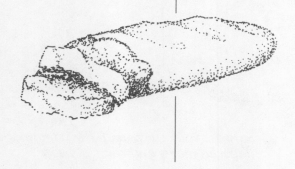

Orange Sponge Cake

Makes 1 (10-inch) cake.

6 eggs, separated
1 cup granulated sugar
1-3/4 cups all-purpose flour
1/2 teaspoon salt
1/3 cup orange juice
1 teaspoon grated orange
    peel
1/2 cup granulated sugar
Sifted powdered sugar

Preheat oven to 350F (175C). In a bowl, beat egg yolks until thick and lemon-colored, about 5 minutes. Gradually beat in 1 cup granulated sugar until smooth. Blend flour and salt; fold into egg-yolk mixture. Fold in orange juice and peel. In a bowl, beat egg whites until foamy. Gradually beat in 1/2 cup granulated sugar. Continue beating until stiff but not dry. Fold egg-yolk mixture into egg-white mixture. Spoon into an ungreased 10-inch tube pan. Bake 35 to 40 minutes or until cake springs back when gently pressed on top. Invert and cool completely in pan. Loosen edges with a spatula; remove from pan. Complete now or make ahead.

To complete now, sprinkle cooled cake with powdered sugar. Place in a cake carrier for transporting. Serve on individual plates.

To make ahead, bake cake up to 2 months ahead; freeze. About 24 hours before serving, thaw at room temperature. Complete and serve as directed above.

1 serving contains:

Cal	Prot	Carb	Fat	Chol	Sodium
203	5g	40g	3g	107mg	120mg

Video Watching

Serves 6 to 8.

Timetable:

- Dragon's Tail Nibbles – Make up to 1 week ahead.
- Minted Tea Ice – Freeze up to 3 days.
- Taste-of-the-Tropics Mold – Make and refrigerate 24 hours.
- Pacific-Rim Pizza – Make topping up to 24 hours ahead.
- Spiced Island Cookies – Bake and freeze up to 1 month.

Shortcuts:

- Serve a combination of fresh and frozen fruits or melons instead of Taste-of-the-Tropics Mold.
- Snack on potato chips, pretzels or nuts instead of Dragon's Tail Nibbles.
- Purchase sherbet or sorbet.
- Purchase cookies.

Dragon's Tail Nibbles

Makes about 3-1/2 cups.

1 cup small pretzel sticks

1 cup crispy chow-mein noodles

1-1/2 cups square rice cereal

2 tablespoons teriyaki sauce

2 tablespoons vegetable oil

1/2 teaspoon ground ginger

1 tablespoon honey

Preheat oven to 300F (150C). In a bowl, combine pretzels, noodles and cereal. In a bowl, combine teriyaki sauce, oil, ginger and honey. Pour over pretzel mixture; toss until well mixed. Spread in a 15" x 10" shallow baking pan. Bake 12 minutes, stirring once.

To complete now, serve in a bowl.

To make ahead, store covered up to 1 week.

1 tablespoon contains:

Cal	Prot	Carb	Fat	Chol	Sodium
16	0	2g	1g	0	50mg

Enjoy an evening at home watching your favorite videos with friends. For convenience, serve this simple delicious meal on individual trays.

Pacific-Rim Pizza

Makes 6 to 8 servings.

1/4 cup coarsely chopped
green onions

2 tablespoons soy sauce

2 tablespoons hoisin sauce

1 tablespoon brown sugar

1 clove garlic

1/4 teaspoon dried
red-pepper flakes

1/3 cup crunchy peanut
butter

2 tablespoons finely
chopped cilantro

2 cups cooked diced
chicken

1/2 cup Chinese pea pods,
halved

1/4 cup chicken broth

1 large carrot, sliced and
cooked

1/3 cup sliced canned
water chestnuts

1 (12-inch) refrigerated
pizza crust, uncooked

In blender or food processor fitted with metal blade, combine green onions, soy sauce, hoisin sauce, brown sugar, garlic and red-pepper flakes. Process until almost smooth. Combine with peanut butter, cilantro, chicken, pea pods, broth, carrot and water chestnuts.

To complete now, preheat oven to 425F (220C). Press pizza crust into 12-inch pizza pan. Bake 10 minutes or until lightly browned. Spoon filling over crust; return to oven for 6 minutes. Serve hot; cut into wedges.

To make ahead, cover and refrigerate toppings up to 24 hours. At serving time, spread mixture on uncooked crust; bake as directed above.

1 serving contains:

Cal	Prot	Carb	Fat	Chol	Sodium
342	17g	32g	17g	29mg	854mg

❖ *Ready in minutes, this pizza with an oriental flare can be eaten out of hand or with a knife and fork.*

Makes 6 to 8 servings.

1 (6-oz.) package
   lemon-flavored gelatin

2 cups boiling water

1-1/2 cups cold water

1 (8-oz.) can crushed
   pineapple in
   unsweetened juice

1 banana, peeled and
   mashed

1 papaya, peeled and cut
   into 12 slices

Sliced oranges or melon,
   if desired

Dissolve gelatin in boiling water; add cold water. Set aside 1-1/2 cups dissolved gelatin. Combine remaining dissolved-gelatin mixture with undrained pineapple and mashed banana; let stand at room temperature. Pour small amount of plain gelatin into 9-inch springform pan. Arrange papaya slices in spoke design; then pour remaining plain gelatin over papaya. Chill until almost firm. Spoon reserved gelatin with fruit over top; chill until set.

To complete now, unmold gelatin on platter; refrigerate until guests arrive. If desired, arrange orange or melon slices around the mold.

To make ahead, cover and refrigerate up to 24 hours. Serve as directed above.

1 serving contains:

Cal	Prot	Carb	Fat	Chol	Sodium
106	2g	26g	0	0	50mg

Minted Tea Ice

Makes about 1 quart.

3 cups water
1/4 cup light corn syrup
1/2 cup butter mints
3 tea bags

In a saucepan, combine water, corn syrup and butter mints. Stir occasionally over medium heat until mixture comes to a boil and mints dissolve. Remove from heat; add tea bags. Cover and steep about 5 minutes. Remove and discard tea bags; cool syrup to room temperature.

To make now, freeze in ice-cream maker according to manufacturer's directions or freeze in refrigerator-freezer until almost solid. Beat in food processor fitted with a metal blade; serve immediately.

To make ahead, freeze according to above directions up to 3 days. Beat in food processor; serve immediately.

1 serving contains:

Cal	Prot	Carb	Fat	Chol	Sodium
111	0	29g	0	0	43mg

❖ *You can serve this refreshing, cool treat in a pretty glass or scoop into ice-cream cones.*

Dim Sum Celebration

❖ *Menu* ❖

Shrimp Dumplings
Pork Potstickers
Mustard Sauce
Barbecued Ribs
Cooked Rice
Chicken Steamed Buns
Tea-Time Custard Tarts

Serves 12.

Timetable:

* Pork Potstickers, Shrimp Dumplings and Chicken Steamed Buns – Fill and freeze up to 1 month.
* Mustard Sauce – Prepare up to 7 days ahead.
* Barbecued Ribs – Marinate ribs at least 4 hours; bake 1-1/2 hours. Refrigerate ribs and marinade up to 24 hours.
* Rice – Cook up to 24 hours ahead.
* Tea-Time Custard Tarts – Bake up to 24 hours ahead.

Shortcuts:

* Purchase 2 or 3 appetizers from Chinese restaurants.
* Purchase mustard sauce.
* Purchase tarts or Chinese almond cookies.

Shrimp Dumplings

Makes about 36 dumplings.

1/2 lb. shrimp, cooked, shelled, deveined, finely chopped

6 water chestnuts, minced

6 mushrooms, finely chopped

1 green onion, finely chopped

1 egg, lightly beaten

1 tablespoon soy sauce

1 tablespoon honey

1/4 teaspoon salt

2 teaspoons sesame oil

36 won-ton skins, cut into 3-inch circles

In a bowl, combine shrimp, water chestnuts, mushrooms and green onion. Stir in egg, soy sauce, honey, salt and oil. Spoon 2 teaspoons mixture into center of each won-ton skin. Pleat edges up around filling. Press pleats together, leaving top open. Cover to prevent drying. Complete now or make ahead.

To complete now, pour water about 1-inch deep in a wok or 12-inch skillet; bring to a boil. Arrange dumplings on a steamer rack in a wok or skillet, open-side up, not touching. Cover and steam over low heat 10 to 15 minutes or until won tons are translucent. Arrange on a serving dish; serve warm.

To make ahead, freeze uncooked dumplings, open-side up, in a single layer on an ungreased baking sheet. Place dumplings in freezer bag. Freeze up to 1 month. About 30 minutes before serving, cook as directed above.

1 dumpling contains:

Cal	Prot	Carb	Fat	Chol	Sodium
16	2g	1g	0	18mg	60mg

Dim Sum translates to heart's delight. Originally these treats were served in Cantonese tea houses. Include a combination of contrasting textures, colors and flavors.

Pork Potstickers

Makes about 36 potstickers.

1 tablespoon cornstarch

2 tablespoons dry white
  wine

1 tablespoon vegetable oil

1/2 lb. lean uncooked
  pork, finely chopped

2 green onions, minced

1 cup minced cabbage

1 tablespoon soy sauce

1 tablespoon brown sugar

1/4 teaspoon salt

1/8 teaspoon pepper

36 won-ton skins, cut into
  3-inch circles

2 tablespoons vegetable oil

1/2 cup chicken broth or
  bouillon

Mustard Sauce, page 96

In a cup, dissolve cornstarch in wine; set aside. In a skillet, heat 1 tablespoon oil. Add pork; stir-fry 3 or 4 minutes. Stir in green onions, cabbage, soy sauce, brown sugar, salt and pepper. Stir cornstarch mixture into pork mixture. Stirring, cook until translucent. Let cool slightly. Spoon 2 teaspoons pork mixture off-center onto each won-ton skin. Moisten edges with water. Bring opposite sides together, forming a semicircle. Pinch edges to seal; make 3 or 4 tucks along sealed edge. Holding a potsticker on tucked edge, place tucked-edge up on a flat surface. Lightly press down until it sits flat. Repeat with remaining skins. Complete now or make ahead.

To complete now, pour 2 tablespoons oil into a 12-inch skillet. Place 6 potstickers in skillet, tucked-edge up, not touching. Cook uncovered until bottoms are golden brown; remove from skillet. Repeat with remaining potstickers. Return browned potstickers to skillet. Pour broth or bouillon into skillet. Cover; cook over low heat 10 minutes or until translucent. Serve warm with Mustard Sauce.

To make ahead, place on a baking sheet and cover. Refrigerate overnight or freeze until firm. Freeze in a freezer bag up to 1 month. About 30 minutes before serving, cook as directed above.

1 potsticker contains:

Cal	Prot	Carb	Fat	Chol	Sodium
28	1g	2g	2g	4mg	47mg

Mustard Sauce

Makes 2/3 cup.

3 tablespoons dry mustard
1/8 teaspoon ground ginger
2 tablespoons hot water
1/4 cup soy sauce
1/2 cup dairy sour cream

In a bowl, combine dry mustard and ginger. Gradually add hot water; stir until smooth. Stir in soy sauce. Spoon sour cream into another bowl. Gradually stir mustard mixture into sour cream; stir until blended. Complete now or make ahead.

To complete now, refrigerate at least 1 hour to let flavors blend.

To make ahead, refrigerate covered up to 7 days.

1 tablespoon contains:

Cal	Prot	Carb	Fat	Chol	Sodium
26	1g	1g	2g	5mg	380mg

❖ *A piquant sauce that's the perfect accent for subtly flavored foods.*

Barbecued Ribs

Makes 12 appetizer servings.

3 to 4 lbs. pork-loin back ribs, halved crosswise

1/3 cup hoisin sauce

3 tablespoons honey

3 tablespoons soy sauce

1 tablespoon sesame oil

3 green onions, minced

1 tablespoon minced ginger root

1 garlic clove, crushed

3 tablespoons wine vinegar

Sesame seeds

Lettuce leaves

Young, tender Chinese pea pods

3 cups cooked rice

Mustard Sauce, page 96

Cut ribs into 1-rib servings; arrange in a single layer in a 13" x 9" baking dish. In a bowl, combine hoisin sauce, honey, soy sauce, sesame oil, green onions, ginger root, garlic and vinegar. Pour over ribs. Cover; refrigerate 4 hours or overnight. Drain; reserve marinade. Arrange ribs in a single layer on broiler rack. Place in cold oven. Pour boiling water in broiler pan until 3/4 full; cover with foil. Bake at 300F (150C) 1-1/2 hours. Complete now or make ahead.

To complete now, remove foil. Increase heat to 350F (175C). Brush ribs with marinade. Bake 35 to 45 minutes or until golden brown. Turn and brush at least once during final baking. Sprinkle tops of ribs with sesame seeds. To serve, line a serving dish with lettuce leaves. Arrange ribs like spokes of a wheel around outer edge. Arrange Chinese pea pods like spokes of a wheel on center, slightly overlapping ribs and lettuce. Spoon rice onto pea pods. Serve hot with Mustard Sauce.

To make ahead, refrigerate baked ribs and reserved marinade separately up to 24 hours. About 1 hour before serving, place ribs in a 13" x 9" baking dish; brush with reserved marinade. Bake 50 to 60 minutes in a 350F (175C) oven, turning and brushing with marinade at least once. Sprinkle tops of ribs with sesame seeds. Serve as directed above.

1 serving contains:

Cal	Prot	Carb	Fat	Chol	Sodium
119	8g	17g	2g	16mg	726mg

Chicken Steamed Buns

Makes 16 steamed buns.

Filling:

2 tablespoons soy sauce

2 tablespoons dry white wine

2 tablespoons hoisin sauce

2 tablespoons ketchup

2 tablespoons honey

1 garlic clove, minced

1 tablespoon minced ginger root

1/4 teaspoon ground allspice or five-spice powder

6 chicken-breast halves, chopped, skinned, boned

2 tablespoons vegetable oil

1/2 cup chicken broth or bouillon

1 tablespoon cornstarch

2 tablespoons water

To make Filling, in a bowl, combine soy sauce, wine, hoisin sauce, ketchup, honey, garlic, ginger root and allspice or five-spice powder. Add chicken and stir. Cover; refrigerate 4 hours. Heat oil in a skillet; add chicken and marinade. Stirring constantly, cook 2 to 3 minutes. Add broth or bouillon. In a cup, dissolve cornstarch in water. Stir into chicken mixture; stirring constantly, cook 3 to 4 minutes or until translucent. Cool; refrigerate.

Prepare Dough. Cut 16 (4-inch) squares of waxed paper; set aside. Punch down dough; let stand 5 minutes. Cut dough in 16 pieces. Shape each into a ball; roll each ball into a 4-inch circle with edges thinner than center. To fill, cup dough in one hand; spoon about 1-1/2 tablespoons filling in center. Gather dough over filling. Twist edges; pinch to seal. If necessary, dampen edge with water. Place buns, sealed-side down, on waxed paper on an ungreased baking sheet. Complete now or make ahead.

Dough:

1 (1/4-oz.) pkg. active dry
 yeast
1 cup warm water
 (110F, 45C)
3 cups all-purpose flour
2 tablespoons sugar
1 tablespoon vegetable oil

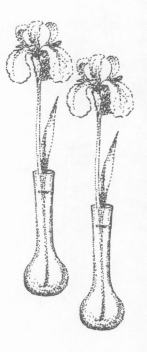

To make Dough, dissolve yeast in water; stir to dissolve. In a bowl, combine flour and sugar. Make a well in center; pour in dissolved yeast and oil. Stir until blended. Turn out onto a lightly floured surface; knead about 5 minutes or until smooth and elastic. Place dough in a greased bowl, turning to coat all sides. Cover with a cloth; let rise in a warm draft-free area about 1 hour or until doubled in bulk.

To complete now, cover buns; let rise until doubled in bulk, about 45 minutes. Pour water 1-inch deep in a wok or 12-inch skillet; bring to a boil. Place buns 1-inch apart on a steamer rack over boiling water; do not crowd. Cover; steam over low heat 20 minutes. Remove waxed paper from cooked buns; serve hot.

To make ahead, freeze buns on waxed paper or baking sheets; then transfer to freezer bags. Freeze up to 1 month. About 2 hours before serving, arrange frozen buns waxed-paper-side down on a baking sheet. Cover with a cloth; let rise in warm draft-free area until doubled in bulk, about 1-1/2 hours. Steam and serve as directed above.

1 bun contains:

Cal	Prot	Carb	Fat	Chol	Sodium
180	13g	23g	3g	26mg	310mg

Tea-Time Custard Tarts

Makes 17 or 18 tarts.

2 cups all-purpose flour

1 teaspoon salt

2/3 cup vegetable shortening

6 to 7 tablespoons water

1 egg white, lightly beaten

1 egg yolk, lightly beaten

3 whole eggs, lightly beaten

2/3 cup sugar

1 (5.33-oz.) can evaporated milk

1/2 cup whole milk

1/2 teaspoon vanilla extract

1/8 teaspoon almond extract

In a bowl, combine flour and salt. Using a pastry blender or 2 knives, cut in shortening until mixture resembles coarse crumbs. Gradually stir in water until mixture forms a ball. On a lightly floured surface, roll dough to 1/8 inch. Cut into 17 or 18 (4-1/2-inch diameter) circles. Preheat oven to 425F (220C). Ease pastry circles into 2-3/4" x 1-1/4" tart pans. Trim edges even with pan rims; brush with egg white. Place pans on a baking sheet. Bake 7 minutes. Remove from oven. Reduce oven temperature to 350F (175C). In a bowl, combine egg yolk, whole eggs and sugar. Stir in milk, vanilla and almond extract. Spoon into baked crusts. Bake 15 to 20 minutes or until a knife inserted in center comes out clean. Cool to room temperature. Complete now or make ahead.

To complete now, arrange cooled tarts on a serving plate.

To make ahead, refrigerate cooled tarts up to 24 hours.

1 tart contains:

Cal	Prot	Carb	Fat	Chol	Sodium
174	4g	19g	9g	49mg	145mg

Bon Voyage Fiesta

❖ Menu ❖

Nachos Grande
Tri-Color Peppers
Corn & Chicken Tamales
Refried Beans
Fresh Salsa
Flour or Corn Tortillas
Carmen's Tropical Flan

Serves 10 to 12.

Timetable:

- Fresh Salsa – Make up to 24 hours ahead.
- Corn & Chicken Tamales – Prepare up to 24 hours ahead.
- Tri-Color Peppers – Make up to 24 hours ahead.
- Carmen's Tropical Flan – Make custard up to 24 hours ahead, but at least 8 hours before serving. Prepare fruits 3 to 4 hours before serving.
- Nachos Grande – Refrigerate 6 to 8 hours.

Shortcuts:

- Use canned refried beans; add cheese before heating.
- Use canned salsa.
- Buy preshredded cheddar cheese and Monterey Jack cheese.

Nachos Grande

Makes 10 to 12 appetizer servings.

4 cups corn-tortilla chips (about 4 oz.)

2 cups shredded Monterey Jack cheese (8 oz.)

1 cup shredded sharp cheddar cheese (4 oz.)

1 (4-oz.) can green chiles, chopped, drained

1/4 cup chopped green onions

1/2 cup dairy sour cream

1/4 cup sliced pitted ripe olives

1 large ripe avocado, chopped, tossed with 1 tablespoon lemon juice

1 tomato, chopped

Chopped cilantro

Taco sauce, if desired

Arrange tortilla chips on a 12-inch pizza pan. Sprinkle with cheeses. Top with chiles and green onions. Complete now or make ahead.

To complete now, place pan 5 to 6 inches from heat; broil 2 to 3 minutes or until cheese melts. Immediately top with sour cream, olives, avocado and tomato. Sprinkle with cilantro. Serve hot with taco sauce, if desired.

To make ahead, cover tightly; refrigerate 6 to 8 hours. Broil, garnish and serve as directed above.

1 serving contains:

Cal	Prot	Carb	Fat	Chol	Sodium
195	9g	8g	15g	31mg	311mg

The flavors and textures of this buffet are designed to satisfy the Mexican-food enthusiast. Accent the buffet table with brightly colored napkins and a large bouquet of paper flowers.

Tri-Color Peppers *(Cover photo)*

Makes 24 wedges.

**1 (8-oz.) pkg. cream
cheese, room
temperature**

1 cup ricotta cheese

**2 teaspoons prepared
horseradish**

**1 teaspoon prepared
mustard**

1/4 teaspoon black pepper

1/2 teaspoon seasoned salt

**1 (2-1/2-oz.) pkg. thinly
sliced smoked or dried
beef, finely chopped**

2 radishes, minced

**1 tablespoon minced green
onion**

**1 medium green bell
pepper**

1 medium red bell pepper

**1 medium yellow bell
pepper**

Halved ripe-olive slices

Pimiento strips

In a bowl, blender or food processor fitted with a metal blade, beat cream cheese, ricotta cheese, horseradish, mustard, black pepper and seasoned salt until smooth. Stir in beef, radishes and green onion; set aside. Remove stems of peppers by cutting a 1-inch circle around tops. Remove seeds from stem; reserve stems. Scoop out seeds and membrane from peppers. Spoon cheese mixture into peppers; top with reserved stems. Wrap each pepper in plastic wrap. Complete now or make ahead.

To complete now, refrigerate at least 2 hours. To serve, remove and discard pepper stems. Cut each pepper in half lengthwise; cut each half into 4 wedges. Arrange on a tray; garnish with olive slices and pimiento strips.

To make ahead, refrigerate up to 24 hours. Cut and serve as directed above.

1 wedge contains:

Cal	Prot	Carb	Fat	Chol	Sodium
54	3g	2g	4g	18mg	190mg

❖ *The vibrant colors in the Mexican flag are repeated in this colorful appetizer.*

Corn & Chicken Tamales

Makes 12 tamales.

9 ears corn in husks or 3 cups frozen corn kernels

3/4 cup yellow cornmeal

3 tablespoons vegetable shortening

2 tablespoons sugar

2 teaspoons salt

3 cups diced cooked chicken

1-1/2 cups diced cheddar cheese (6 oz.)

1/3 cup minced canned green chiles

1 tablespoon minced onion

Remove husks and silk from corn, reserving 40 to 60 of largest husks. Cut kernels off cobs; discard cobs. In blender or food processor fitted with a metal blade, process corn until finely chopped. In a bowl, combine chopped corn, cornmeal, shortening, sugar and salt. Stir until blended. In a bowl, combine chicken, cheese, chiles and onion. Place 2 or 3 corn husks on a flat surface with long edges overlapping. Spread 3 tablespoons corn in center of husks making a 5" x 4" rectangle. Top with 1/3 cup chicken. Spread another 3 tablespoons corn over chicken. Fold husks over filling, overlapping to encase filling. Tie open ends of husks with string. Repeat. Complete now or make ahead.

To complete now, pour 1 inch of water in a Dutch oven or kettle with a rack; lay tamales flat on rack, overlapping if necessary. Cover and steam 60 to 70 minutes or until tamales are firm when touched. Remove from pot; serve hot in husks.

To make ahead, refrigerate up to 24 hours. Steam tamales about 1-1/2 hours; serve as directed above.

1 tamale contains:

Cal	Prot	Carb	Fat	Chol	Sodium
250	16g	24g	11g	44mg	516mg

If corn is husked, purchase dried husks. Soak in hot water 1 hour to soften. Tamales can be prepared in foil rather than husks. Cut 12 (9" x 7") pieces of foil. Spread with corn and chicken as directed above. Fold foil over filling. Fold edges twice to make a secure package. Stand tamales, folded-edge down, on a rack. Cover and steam 1 hour or until dough pulls away from foil easily.

Fresh Salsa

Makes 1-1/2 cups.

2 fresh green chiles

1 large tomato, chopped

1 onion, chopped

1/4 cup loosely packed chopped cilantro

1/2 teaspoon salt

2 tablespoons white vinegar

1/2 teaspoon celery seeds

To handle fresh chiles, wear rubber or plastic gloves. After handling, do not touch your face or eyes. Cut chiles in thin strips; discard seeds. Finely chop chiles. In a bowl, combine chopped chiles, tomato, onion, cilantro, salt, vinegar and celery seeds. Cover. Complete now or make ahead.

To complete now, refrigerate at least 2 hours to let flavors blend; serve cold.

To make ahead, refrigerate up to 24 hours.

1 tablespoon contains:

Cal	Prot	Carb	Fat	Chol	Sodium
6	0	1g	0	0	45mg

Carmen's Tropical Flan

Makes 10 to 12 servings.

3/4 cup sugar

6 eggs, lightly beaten

3 cups milk or half and half

1/3 cup sugar

1/2 cup flaked coconut

1 teaspoon vanilla extract

2 papayas, peeled, sliced, seeded

1 pineapple, cubed, peeled

2 kiwi fruit, sliced, peeled

In a heavy skillet, heat 3/4 cup sugar, stirring constantly until melted and golden. Immediately pour into bottom of a 9-inch cake pan; set aside. Preheat oven to 325F (165C). In a bowl combine eggs, milk or half and half, 1/3 cup sugar, coconut and vanilla. Pour over sugar in pan. Place pan in a 13" x 10" pan. Pour water about 1-inch deep in bottom pan. Bake 40 to 45 minutes or until a knife inserted off-center comes out clean. Remove from water; let stand 15 minutes. Cover. Complete now or make ahead.

To complete now, refrigerate 8 hours. To serve, loosen edges with a spatula. Invert onto a large serving plate; remove pan. Garnish with fruits. Serve cold.

To make ahead, refrigerate up to 24 hours. Garnish and serve as directed above.

1 serving contains:

Cal	Prot	Carb	Fat	Chol	Sodium
197	6g	34g	5g	112mg	72mg

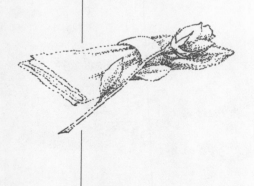

Tropical Dream

Serves 6.

Timetable:

- Trade-Winds Cake – Make up to 24 hours ahead. Glaze and slice 3 hours before serving.
- South-Seas Loaf – Make up to 24 hours ahead.
- Mariner's Filo Roll-Ups – Fill and roll up to 24 hours ahead.
- Oasis Coleslaw – Prepare cabbage, fruit and dressing up to 24 hours ahead.
- Sesame Chicken Wings – Make up to 24 hours ahead.
- Caribbean Connection – Combine juice, coconut syrup and liqueurs up to 24 hours ahead.

Shortcuts:

- Purchase coleslaw.
- Purchase date-nut bread or orange bread.
- Make a coconut cake from a mix.

Makes 6 servings.

2 cups pineapple juice

6 tablespoons cream of coconut

6 tablespoons almond-flavored liqueur

1/4 cup orange-flavored liqueur

Orange wedges

Fresh pineapple wedges

Fresh strawberries

1 banana

1-1/2 cups crushed ice

In a 2-quart pitcher, combine pineapple juice, cream of coconut and liqueurs. Complete now or make ahead.

To complete now, thread orange, pineapple and strawberries on 6-inch skewers; set aside. Pour juice mixture into a blender. Add banana and ice. Process until smooth. Immediately pour into tall wine or champagne glasses. Place 1 fruit skewer in each glass.

To make ahead, combine juice, syrup and liqueurs; cover and refrigerate up to 24 hours. Thread fruit on skewers. Wrap in plastic wrap; refrigerate 6 to 8 hours. Complete as directed above.

1 serving contains:

Cal	Prot	Carb	Fat	Chol	Sodium
195	1g	28g	3g	0	5mg

An elegant informal supper featuring flavors of the islands. Delicate seafood flavors enchance Mariner's Filo Roll-Ups. For a tropical look, buy ti leaves and fresh flowers.

Sesame Chicken Wings

Makes 36 to 40 appetizers.

4 lbs. chicken wings

2/3 cup all-purpose flour

2 eggs, lightly beaten

2 tablespoons water

1-1/3 cups finely crushed round rich crackers

1-1/3 cups grated Parmesan cheese (2 oz.)

1-1/3 cups sesame seeds, toasted

1/4 cup minced fresh parsley

1 teaspoon seasoned pepper

2 teaspoons seasoned salt

1/4 cup butter or margarine, melted

Remove and discard wing tips. Cut wings apart at joints. Pour flour into a shallow dish. In another shallow dish, beat eggs with water. In a bowl, combine cracker crumbs, Parmesan cheese, sesame seeds, parsley, pepper and salt. Preheat oven to 375F (190C). Pour melted butter or margarine into a 13" x 9" baking pan. Roll chicken in flour, then in egg; then in crumb mixture. Arrange chicken in a single layer in baking pan. Bake 45 minutes. Complete now or make ahead.

To complete now, place hot wings on a plate and serve. Or drain on paper towels; cool slightly. Cover; refrigerate until chilled. Chicken can be served warm or cold.

To make ahead, drain baked chicken on paper towels. Refrigerate covered up to 24 hours. Serve warm or cold. To warm, place in baking pan; heat at 375F (190C) 15 to 20 minutes.

1 appetizer contains:

Cal	Prot	Carb	Fat	Chol	Sodium
173	11g	3g	13g	51mg	220mg

❖ *A delicious coating that's bound to win you over after the first bite.*

Mariner's Filo Roll-Ups

1 cup cooked, flaked crabmeat (6 oz.)

1/2 cup chopped mushrooms

1 tablespoon minced fresh parsley

1/4 teaspoon dried dill weed

1/2 teaspoon salt

1/4 teaspoon pepper

1 cup soft breadcrumbs

6 sole fillets

12 filo sheets

1/2 cup butter, melted

In a bowl, combine crabmeat, mushrooms, parsley, dill weed, salt, pepper and breadcrumbs. Spoon mixture onto centers of sole fillets. Fold ends of fillets over filling, overlapping ends. Keep filo sheets covered until needed to prevent drying. Brush butter on 1 filo sheet. Top with a second filo sheet; brush with butter. Fold buttered filo sheets in half. Place 1 stuffed sole fillet in center of filo. Fold long sides of filo over top, slightly overlapping. Fold ends, overlapping, over fillet. Place seam-side down in an ungreased 13" x 9" baking dish. Brush with butter. Repeat with remaining fish fillets. Complete now or make ahead.

To complete now, bake at 375F (190C) 25 to 30 minutes or until filo is golden brown. Arrange roll-ups on a serving dish; serve hot.

To make ahead, cover and refrigerate up to 24 hours. Bake and serve as directed above.

1 serving contains:

Cal	Prot	Carb	Fat	Chol	Sodium
359	31g	18g	18g	121mg	533mg

❖ *Delicately flavored seafood is wrapped in filo and baked to a beautiful golden brown.*

Oasis Coleslaw

Makes 5 or 6 servings.

1/2 medium head cabbage, shredded

2 navel oranges, peeled, diced

1/2 cup chopped dates

1/2 cup dairy sour cream

1/4 teaspoon dry mustard

1 tablespoon honey

2 teaspoons minced crystallized ginger

1/2 teaspoon salt

1/8 teaspoon pepper

In a bowl, combine cabbage, oranges and dates. In a bowl, combine sour cream, dry mustard, honey, crystallized ginger, salt and pepper. Complete now or make ahead.

To complete now, pour dressing over cabbage mixture and toss. Spoon into a serving bowl.

To make ahead, cover and refrigerate cabbage mixture and sour-cream dressing separately up to 24 hours. Complete as directed above.

1 serving contains:

Cal	Prot	Carb	Fat	Chol	Sodium
125	2g	23g	4g	9mg	195mg

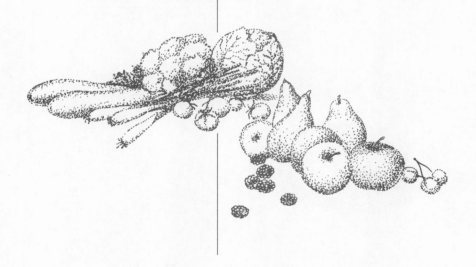

South-Seas Loaf

3/4 cup whole-wheat flour

3/4 cup all-purpose flour

1/4 teaspoon salt

2 teaspoons baking powder

1 teaspoon baking soda

2 eggs, lightly beaten

2 tablespoons vegetable oil

1/3 cup honey

3/4 cup whole-bran cereal

3/4 cup dairy sour cream

1 large ripe mango, peeled, puréed

1 teaspoon grated orange peel

1/3 cup flaked coconut

Grease a 9" x 5" loaf pan; set aside. Preheat oven to 350F (175C). In a bowl, combine flours, salt, baking powder and baking soda. In another bowl, combine eggs, oil, honey, whole-bran cereal, sour cream, mango, orange peel and coconut. Add egg mixture to dry ingredients. Stir enough to moisten. Spoon into greased pan; smooth top. Bake 40 to 45 minutes or until a wooden pick inserted in center comes out clean. Cool in pan on a wire rack 10 minutes. Turn out onto rack; cool completely. Complete now or make ahead.

To complete now, let bread stand about 2 hours. Slice and arrange on a serving plate.

To make ahead, make up to 24 hours ahead. Wrap cooled bread. About 3 hours before serving, slice bread; arrange on a platter or serving plate. Cover and refrigerate until served.

1 slice contains:

Cal	Prot	Carb	Fat	Chol	Sodium
179	4g	27g	7g	42mg	221mg

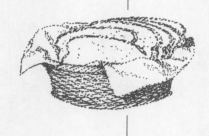

Trade-Winds Cake

Makes 1 (10-inch) cake.

3 eggs

3/4 cup vegetable oil

1 cup sugar

1/2 cup cream of coconut

1 (8-oz.) can crushed
  pineapple in syrup

2 tablespoons almond-
  flavored liqueur

1 teaspoon grated orange
  peel

3 cups all-purpose flour

2 teaspoons baking powder

1 teaspoon baking soda

Glaze:

2 teaspoons cornstarch

2 tablespoons sugar

1/4 cup orange juice

1 tablespoon almond-
  flavored liqueur

Grease and flour a 10-inch tube pan; set aside. Preheat oven to 350F (175C). In a bowl, beat eggs lightly. Add oil, 1 cup sugar and cream of coconut; beat until thick and foamy. Drain pineapple, reserving 1/2 cup syrup for glaze. To egg mixture, add drained pineapple, 2 tablespoons liqueur and orange peel. In a bowl, combine flour, baking powder and baking soda; stir into egg mixture. Pour into prepared pan. Bake 45 to 55 minutes or until a wooden pick inserted off-center comes out clean. Let stand in pan 10 minutes. Invert onto a rack; remove pan and cool. Complete now or make ahead.

To make Glaze, in a saucepan, combine cornstarch, 2 tablespoons sugar, reserved pineapple syrup and orange juice. Stirring, cook until thickened. Stir in 1 tablespoon liqueur; cool 5 minutes.

To complete now, spoon warm glaze over cake. Let stand until glaze sets. Slice and serve.

To make ahead, bake cake up to 24 hours ahead; cover. Prepare glaze; brush over cake 2 to 3 hours before serving. Cover.

1 serving contains:

Cal	Prot	Carb	Fat	Chol	Sodium
378	5g	50g	17g	53mg	141mg

Mediterranean Fare

❖ *Menu* ❖

Mediterranean Kabobs
Three-Way Gnocchi
Mixed Green Salad
Provençal Zucchini Bake
Rosy Raspberry Pears
Brie Cheese

Serves 6 to 8.

Timetable:

- Mediterranean Kabobs – Cover lamb with herbs; refrigerate up to 24 hours.
- Three-Way Gnocchi – Make gnocchi and sauces up to 24 hours ahead.
- Provençal Zucchini Bake – Make up to 24 hours ahead. Bake zucchini before broiling meat.
- Rosy Raspberry Pears – Make up to 24 hours ahead.

Shortcuts:

- Serve steamed or sautéed zucchini instead of Provençal Zucchini Bake.
- Omit Three-Way Gnocchi, substitute minestrone soup.

Mediterranean Kabobs

Makes 8 servings.

1 tablespoon chopped
   fresh thyme or
   1 teaspoon dried-leaf
   thyme

1 tablespoon chopped
   fresh rosemary or
   1 teaspoon dried
   rosemary

1 garlic clove, crushed

1 teaspoon grated lemon
   peel

1 teaspoon salt

1/4 teaspoon pepper

2 teaspoons Dijon-style
   mustard

1/4 cup lemon juice

1/2 cup olive oil or
   vegetable oil

2-1/2 to 3 lbs. boned leg of
   lamb, cut in 1-1/2-inch
   cubes

In a shallow 10" x 6" baking dish, blend together all ingredients except lamb. Add lamb, turning to coat. Cover. Complete now or make ahead.

To complete now, refrigerate at least 2 hours. Drain, reserving marinade. Thread lamb cubes on 8 skewers. Place on a broiler pan; brush with reserved marinade. Broil 4 to 5 inches from heat 3 to 4 minutes on each side, brushing with marinade. Serve hot.

To make ahead, refrigerate up to 24 hours. Broil as directed above.

1 serving contains:

Cal	Prot	Carb	Fat	Chol	Sodium
260	20g	1g	20g	63mg	331mg

This vibrant menu brings together some of our favorite country dishes from the Mediterranean. Poached Rosy Raspberry Pears and cheese complete a delicious meal.

115

Three-Way Gnocchi

Makes 6 to 8 servings.

**6 mashed, peeled, baked
  potatoes**

1 teaspoon salt

**1-1/4 to 1-1/2 cups
  all-purpose flour**

**1/4 cup butter or
  margarine, melted**

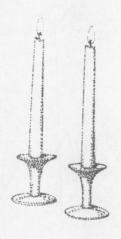

In a bowl, combine mashed potatoes, salt and
enough flour to make a stiff dough. Turn out
onto a lightly floured surface. Knead lightly,
work in flour to make dough smooth. Divide
into egg-size pieces. Shape each piece into a
1/2-inch-thick log; cut into 1-inch lengths. With
fork tines, make light crosswise depressions in
each. In a pot, bring 3 quarts lightly salted water
to a boil. Add about 1/4 of gnocchi to water.
After gnocchi float to top of water, cook 10
seconds. Remove cooked gnocchi; drain briefly.
Stir into shallow bowl of butter or margarine.
Divide into 3 shallow casserole dishes. Make
Toppings.

To complete now, cover dishes. Bake at 350F
(175C) 15 to 20 minutes or until bubbly; garnish
Pesto Topping with basil sprig and Gorgonzola
Topping with 1 teaspoon minced parsley. Serve
hot.

To make ahead, cover and refrigerate prepared
dishes up to 24 hours. Bake covered dishes at
350F (175C) 20 to 25 minutes or until bubbly.
Garnish as directed above.

1 serving without Topping contains:

Cal	Prot	Carb	Fat	Chol	Sodium
231	4g	40g	6g	16mg	321mg

Gorgonzola Topping:

2 tablespoons grated
   Parmesan cheese

2 oz. Gorgonzola cheese,
   crumbled

2 tablespoons half and half

2 teaspoons minced fresh
   parsley

Almond-Brie Topping:

2 oz. Brie cheese, cubed

1/4 cup half and half

2 tablespoons sliced
   almonds

Pesto Topping:

1 medium tomato, peeled,
   seeded, chopped

1/4 cup chopped fresh
   basil leaves or 1/2
   teaspoon dried-leaf basil

1/4 cup ricotta cheese

1 garlic clove, crushed

2 tablespoons chopped
   pine nuts

1/4 teaspoon salt

2 tablespoons grated
   Parmesan cheese

Basil sprig

Gorgonzola Topping: In a bowl, combine cheeses, half and half and 1 teaspoon minced parsley. Spread over one dish of gnocchi.

1 serving contains:

Cal	Prot	Carb	Fat	Chol	Sodium
134	8g	1g	11g	30mg	533mg

Almond-Brie Topping: Sprinkle Brie over gnocchi and pour half and half over top. Sprinkle with almonds.

1 serving contains:

Cal	Prot	Carb	Fat	Chol	Sodium
147	7g	2g	13g	34mg	166mg

Pesto Topping: In blender or food processor fitted with a metal blade, combine all ingredients except basil sprig. Process until finely chopped. Pour over gnocchi.

1 serving contains:

Cal	Prot	Carb	Fat	Chol	Sodium
211	8g	9g	19g	12mg	370mg

Provençal Zucchini Bake

6 to 8 medium zucchini, cut in 3/8-inch diagonal slices

2 teaspoons salt

1/4 cup vegetable oil

1 large onion, chopped

8 tomatoes, peeled, seeded, chopped

1 garlic clove, crushed

1/2 teaspoon dried-leaf basil

1/4 teaspoon salt

1/8 teaspoon pepper

1/4 cup beef broth or bouillon

1 cup dairy sour cream

1 egg, lightly beaten

1/2 cup grated Parmesan cheese (1-1/2 oz.)

Sprinkle zucchini with 2 teaspoons salt. Place in a colander; let stand 2 hours. Rinse; drain and pat dry with paper towels. In a skillet, heat oil; add zucchini. Cook 5 minutes. Drain on paper towels. Add onion to skillet and sauté. Stir in tomatoes, garlic, basil, 1/4 teaspoon salt and pepper. Simmer 30 to 40 minutes until thickened. Spoon 1 cup tomato mixture into a bowl. Stir in broth or bouillon. Reserve remaining tomato sauce. In another bowl, combine sour cream and egg; set aside. Overlap zucchini slices on bottom and side of a 1-quart charlotte mold. Top with 3 tablespoons tomato mixture, 1/3 of sour-cream mixture and 1/3 of cheese. Continue layering zucchini, tomato, sour cream and cheese, ending with zucchini. Cover filled mold with foil. Complete now or make ahead.

To complete now, bake covered at 350F (175C) 45 to 50 minutes. Remove from oven; let stand 10 minutes. Heat reserved tomato sauce. Pour into a serving bowl; keep hot. Invert mold onto a serving plate; remove mold. Serve heated sauce separately.

To make ahead, refrigerate covered mold and reserved tomato sauce separately up to 24 hours. Bake covered at 350F (175C) 55 to 60 minutes. Heat tomato sauce and serve as directed above.

1 serving contains:

Cal	Prot	Carb	Fat	Chol	Sodium
198	6g	11g	16g	43mg	730mg

Rosy Raspberry Pears

Makes 4 servings.

3 cups raspberry-cranberry-juice drink

1 (3-inch) cinnamon stick

4 whole cloves

1/4 cup sugar

2 unpeeled lemon slices

4 large ripe pears

1/4 cup black-raspberry liqueur

In a large skillet, combine juice drink, cinnamon stick, cloves, sugar and lemon slices. Bring to a boil. Peel, halve and core pears. Carefully place pears into boiling liquid. Cover and simmer 8 to 10 minutes until pears are tender. Remove from heat; stir in liqueur. Place pears and juice in a bowl. Cover. Complete now or make ahead.

To complete now, refrigerate at least 2 hours. To serve, remove cinnamon stick and cloves; spoon pears and juice into individual dessert dishes.

To make ahead, refrigerate up to 24 hours. Serve as directed above.

1 serving contains:

Cal	Prot	Carb	Fat	Chol	Sodium
336	1g	77g	1g	0	6mg

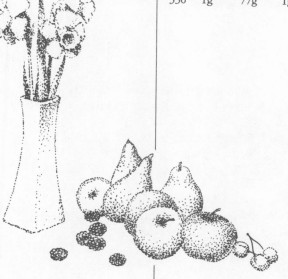

❖ *If using Bosc pears cook a few minutes longer or until tender.*

119

Chocolate Splurge

❖ *Menu* ❖

Fudge-Nut Truffles
Hazelnut Dream
Chocolate Cheesecake
Fudge Mousse Cake
Choco-Macadamia Tart

Serves 10 to 12.

Timetable:

- Hazelnut Dream – Freeze baked cake up to 1 month. Make filling up to 24 hours ahead. Fill and glaze cake on day of party.
- Fudge-Mousse Cake – Freeze baked cake up to 1 month. Make mousse up to 24 hours ahead.
- Fudge-Nut Truffles – Make and freeze up to 1 month. Or refrigerate up to 4 days.
- Chocolate Cheesecake – Make 24 hours ahead.
- Choco-Macadamia Tart – Best when made on day it's served; may be made up to 24 hours ahead.

Shortcuts:

- Purchase chocolate cake or cheesecake.
- Purchase truffles.

Fudge-Nut Truffles

Makes 24 truffles.

**1 (12-oz.) pkg. semi-sweet
chocolate pieces (2 cups)**

**3/4 cup sweetened
condensed milk**

1 teaspoon vanilla extract

**1 cup finely chopped
walnuts or pecans**

In top of a double boiler, melt chocolate over hot water. Stir in condensed milk and vanilla. Spoon into a shallow dish; refrigerate 10 to 15 minutes or until firm enough to shape. Place nuts in a pie plate. With a teaspoon, scoop chilled chocolate mixture; with another teaspoon, push mixture from spoon into nuts. Roll in nuts and shape in a ball. Place in a bon-bon cup. Repeat with remaining chocolate and nuts. Complete now or make ahead.

To complete now, refrigerate 15 minutes before serving.

To make ahead, cover and refrigerate up to 4 days. Freeze up to 1 month. Thaw in refrigerator. Remove 15 minutes before serving.

1 truffle contains:

Cal	Prot	Carb	Fat	Chol	Sodium
134	2g	14g	9g	3mg	15mg

Celebrate the love of chocolate! If your idea of heaven is to indulge in divine chocolate desserts, our mouth-watering, distinctive desserts will delight you.

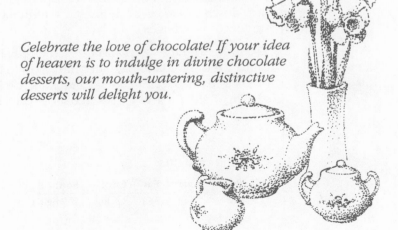

Hazelnut Dream

Makes 1 (9-inch) cake.

4 eggs

3/4 cup sugar

1/2 teaspoon vanilla extract

2/3 cup all-purpose flour

1/2 cup unsweetened
cocoa powder

1/4 cup butter, melted

Hazelnut-Butter Filling:

2 cups hazelnuts, roasted
and rubbed

1/4 cup light corn syrup

1/4 cup butter, room
temperature

1 cup sifted powdered
sugar

Satiny Chocolate Glaze:

6 oz. semi-sweet chocolate

2 teaspoons vegetable oil

1/4 cup butter, room
temperature

Grease and flour a 9-inch round cake pan. Preheat oven to 375F (190C). In a bowl, beat eggs, sugar and vanilla until thick, about 5 minutes. Combine flour and cocoa powder in a sifter. Sift about 1/3 of flour at a time into egg mixture; fold in after each addition. Fold in butter. Spoon into pan. Bake 25 to 30 minutes or until a wooden pick inserted in center comes out clean. Cool in pan 5 minutes. Invert and remove pan. Cool. Complete now or make ahead.

To make Hazelnut-Butter Filling, pour nuts into blender or food processor. Process until nuts are peanut-butter consistency. Add corn syrup; process until blended. In a bowl, beat butter and powdered sugar until light and fluffy. Stir in hazelnut mixture.

To make Satiny Chocolate Glaze, in a heavy saucepan, combine chocolate, oil and butter. Stir constantly over low heat until chocolate melts.

To complete now, prepare Hazelnut-Butter Filling and Satiny Chocolate Glaze. Slice cake in half horizontally. Place 1 layer, cut-side up, on a cake plate. Spread with filling. Top with remaining layer. Pour glaze over top and allow to drip down sides. Let set at least 15 minutes. To serve, cut in wedges.

To make ahead, wrap and freeze baked cake up to 1 month. Make hazelnut filling up to 24 hours ahead. Cover. Make glaze just before serving. Split, fill and glaze cake as directed above.

1 serving contains:

Cal	Prot	Carb	Fat	Chol	Sodium
552	8g	53g	38g	122mg	149mg

Chocolate Cheesecake

Makes 8 to 10 servings.

1-3/4 cups chocolate-wafer
   crumbs

1 tablespoon sugar

2 tablespoons butter or
   margarine, melted

2 (8-oz.) pkgs. cream
   cheese, room
   temperature

1 cup cottage cheese

1-1/4 cups sugar

3 eggs, lightly beaten

1 teaspoon vanilla extract

1 cup whipping cream

1/2 cup unsweetened
   cocoa powder, sifted

1/2 teaspoon ground
   cinnamon

1 cup dairy sour cream

2 tablespoons sugar

Chocolate Leaves:

1 oz. semi-sweet chocolate

In a bowl, combine crumbs, 1 tablespoon sugar and butter or margarine. Press over bottom and 1-1/2 inches up side of a 9-inch springform pan. Refrigerate. Preheat oven to 350F (175C). In a bowl, combine cream cheese, cottage cheese and sugar; beat until smooth. Beat in eggs and vanilla. In a bowl, whip cream until soft peaks form; fold into cheese mixture. Spoon 1/2 of filling into crumb-lined pan. Stir cocoa powder and cinnamon into remaining cheese mixture. Drop by spoonfuls on top of cheese filling. Pull a spatula through fillings making a zigzag pattern; do not disturb crust. Bake 65 to 70 minutes or until firm around edge and center jiggles slightly. Center sets up as it cools. Turn off oven; leave in oven with door ajar 1 hour. Refrigerate at least 2 hours. Complete now or make ahead.

To complete now, prepare Chocolate Leaves. In a bowl, combine sour cream and 2 tablespoons sugar. Spread sour-cream mixture over cheesecake. Top with a circle of chocolate leaves; refrigerate. To serve, cut in wedges.

To make Chocolate Leaves, choose nonpoisonous leaves, such as rose or geranium. Rinse and pat dry. Melt chocolate; brush about 1/8-inch thick on underside of leaves, just to edge. Place coated-side up and refrigerate until firm. Peel leaves away from chocolate and discard.

To make ahead, bake crust and filling up to 1 month ahead. Wrap and freeze. Thaw overnight in refrigerator. Add sour-cream mixture and leaves 24 hours before or early on day of party.

1 serving contains:

Cal	Prot	Carb	Fat	Chol	Sodium
565	11g	47g	39g	175mg	327mg

Fudge-Mousse Cake (Cover Photo)

Makes 8 to 10 servings.

2 eggs
1 cup sugar
1/2 cup butter or margarine, melted
3/4 cup all-purpose flour
1/4 cup unsweetened cocoa powder, sifted
1/2 teaspoon vanilla extract

Mousse:
1 (1/4-oz.) envelope unflavored gelatin
1 cup milk
3 eggs
3/4 cup sugar
1 teaspoon vanilla extract
1 cup whipping cream
1/4 cup sugar

3 oz. semi-sweet chocolate

Whipped cream, if desired
Chocolate curls or slivers, if desired

Preheat oven to 350F (175C). Grease a 9-inch springform pan; set aside. In a bowl, beat 2 eggs until thick, about 5 minutes. Beat in sugar. Stir in butter or margarine, flour, cocoa powder and vanilla. Pour into greased pan; bake 25 to 30 minutes or until cake pulls away from pan edge. Cool in pan. Complete now or make ahead.

To make Mousse, in a saucepan, sprinkle gelatin over milk; let stand 5 minutes. In a bowl beat eggs and 3/4 cup sugar about 5 minutes. Stir eggs into milk mixture. Stirring, cook over low heat until thickened. Remove from heat; stir in vanilla. Cool; refrigerate about 1 hour, or until mixture begins to set, stirring once. In a bowl, beat whipping cream until soft peaks form, beat in 1/4 cup sugar. Fold whipped cream into egg mixture.

To complete now, prepare Mousse. Spoon 1/2 of white mousse mixture over cake in pan; keep remaining half cool, but do not refrigerate. Refrigerate cake about 1 hour or until mousse is firm. Melt chocolate; set aside to cool slightly. Stir chocolate into reserved mousse; spoon over mixture in cake pan. Cover and refrigerate at least 4 hours. Remove side of springform pan. Garnish with whipped cream and chocolate curls or slivers, if desired. Refrigerate.

To make ahead, wrap and freeze baked cake up to 1 month. Up to 24 hours before party, make and add mousse layers as directed above.

1 serving contains:

Cal	Prot	Carb	Fat	Chol	Sodium
452	7g	55g	25g	166mg	132mg

Choco-Macadamia Tart

Makes 1 (9-inch) tart.

1 cup all-purpose flour
1/2 teaspoon salt
1/3 cup vegetable
shortening
3 to 4 tablespoons water

Filling:
1 cup macadamia nuts
3 eggs, lightly beaten
3/4 cup light corn syrup
1/4 cup butter or
margarine, melted
3/4 cup lightly packed
brown sugar
1/2 teaspoon vanilla extract

1 oz. semi-sweet chocolate

In a bowl, combine flour and salt. Cut in shortening until mixture resembles coarse crumbs. Gradually stir in water until mixture forms a ball. On a lightly floured surface, roll out dough to an 11-inch circle; line a 9-inch tart or quiche pan. Trim edges and refrigerate. Preheat oven to 375F (190C). Prepare Filling. Spoon Filling into pastry-lined pan. Bake 35 to 40 minutes or until a wooden pick inserted in center comes out clean and filling is firm in center. If crust browns too quickly, cover edges with foil. Cool. Melt chocolate and drizzle over tart. Complete now or make ahead.

To make Filling, coarsely chop nuts in a food processor fitted with a metal blade. In a bowl, combine eggs, corn syrup, butter or margarine, brown sugar and vanilla; beat until blended. Stir in chopped nuts.

To complete now, cut in wedges; serve immediately.

To make ahead, refrigerate tart up to 24 hours.

1 serving contains:

Cal	Prot	Carb	Fat	Chol	Sodium
407	4g	48g	24g	76mg	183mg

❖ *Indulge yourself and savor this heavenly dessert.*

Deli Razzle-Dazzle

❖ *Menu* ❖

Mustard-Cream Mold
Hot Potato Salad
Garden Medley
Peppered Brioche Loaf
Prepared Mustards
Rhineland Relish
Pickled Beets & Cucumbers
Fruit Compote

Serves 6 to 8.

Timetable:

- Peppered Brioche Loaf – Make and freeze up to 1 month. Or refrigerate up to 2 days.
- Mustard-Cream Mold – Make up to 24 hours ahead.
- Rhineland Relish – Make up to 24 hours ahead.
- Pickled Beets & Cucumbers – Make up to 24 hours ahead.
- Garden Medley – Marinate up to 24 hours.
- Hot Potato Salad – Cook potatoes and bacon and prepare dressing up to 24 hours ahead.

Shortcuts:

- Purchase breads, specialty mustards, cold cuts, cheeses and salads.

Mustard-Cream Mold (Cover photo)

Makes about 3 cups.

1/2 cup sugar

1 (1/4-oz.) envelope unflavored gelatin

1/2 cup white-wine vinegar

1 cup water

2 eggs, lightly beaten

2 tablespoons Dijon-style mustard

1 tablespoon prepared horseradish

1/2 teaspoon grated onion

1 cup dairy sour cream

Curly lettuce leaves

Endive

Pimiento-stuffed green-olive slices

Assorted sliced cold meats

Assorted sliced cheeses

In a saucepan, combine sugar and gelatin. Add vinegar and water. Stir constantly over heat until sugar dissolves. Remove from heat. Stir 1/2 cup hot mixture into eggs. Stir eggs into remaining hot mixture. Stirring constantly, cook over low heat until thickened. Remove from heat. Stir in mustard, horseradish, onion and sour cream. Pour into a 4-cup mold and cover. Complete now or make ahead.

To complete now, refrigerate at least 4 hours. Line a serving plate with lettuce leaves. Invert mold onto lettuce; remove mold. Garnish with endive and green-olive slices. Arrange cold meats and cheeses around mold. Serve immediately.

To make ahead, refrigerate up to 24 hours. Garnish and serve as directed above.

1 tablespoon contains:

Cal	Prot	Carb	Fat	Chol	Sodium
23	1g	3g	1g	11mg	14mg

The perfect informal menu for spur-of-the-moment entertaining. You can prepare some foods and purchase others. Served in stemmed goblets, fruit compote becomes a visual delight.

Hot Potato Salad

6 large potatoes, peeled, cooked

4 bacon slices, chopped

1 onion, chopped

1/4 cup all-purpose flour

2 tablespoons sugar

4 teaspoons Dijon-style mustard

1 tablespoon lemon juice

3 tablespoons white-wine vinegar

3/4 teaspoon salt

1/8 teaspoon pepper

1 cup water

1/4 teaspoon celery seeds

2 hard-cooked eggs, sliced

Cut potatoes into 1/2-inch cubes. Place in a bowl; keep warm. In a skillet, cook bacon until crisp; drain on paper towels. Reserve drippings in skillet. Crumble drained bacon; set aside. In hot bacon drippings, sauté onion. Stir in flour and sugar until blended. Stir in mustard, lemon juice, vinegar, salt, pepper, water and celery seeds. Stirring constantly, cook over medium heat 2 to 3 minutes until thickened. Complete now or make ahead.

To complete now, pour vinegar mixture over potatoes and toss to coat. Spoon into a salad bowl. Garnish with crumbled bacon and egg slices; serve hot.

To make ahead, cook, peel and cube potatoes and slice eggs 24 hours ahead. Cover and refrigerate. Cook, drain and crumble bacon; refrigerate up to 24 hours. Prepare dressing as directed above and refrigerate up to 24 hours. To serve, combine potatoes and dressing in a skillet. Stir over low heat until heated through. Garnish and serve as directed above.

1 serving contains:

Cal	Prot	Carb	Fat	Chol	Sodium
229	8g	39g	5g	79mg	497mg

Garden Medley

Makes 6 servings.

**2 yellow crookneck
squash, thinly sliced**

2 zucchini, thinly sliced

12 cherry tomatoes, halved

**1/2 cup olive oil or
vegetable oil**

1/4 cup tarragon vinegar

1 tablespoon lemon juice

**2 teaspoons Dijon-style
mustard**

**1 tablespoon minced green
onion**

**2 tablespoons minced
watercress leaves**

**1/4 teaspoon dried-leaf
chervil**

1/2 teaspoon salt

1/4 teaspoon pepper

Lettuce leaves

In a bowl, combine crookneck squash, zucchini
and tomatoes. In a cup combine oil, vinegar,
lemon juice, mustard, green onion, watercress,
chervil, salt and pepper. Pour over vegetables;
toss to coat. Cover. Complete now or make
ahead.

To complete now, refrigerate at least 2 hours.
Line a serving bowl with lettuce leaves. Drain
marinade. Spoon vegetables into bowl; serve
cold.

To make ahead, refrigerate up to 24 hours.
Drain and serve as directed above.

1 serving contains:

Cal	Prot	Carb	Fat	Chol	Sodium
182	1g	5g	18g	0	205mg

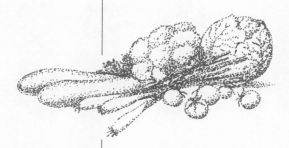

❖ *A colorful celebration of fresh vegetables
marinated in a French-inspired dressing.*

Peppered Brioche Loaf

Makes 1 (9" x 5") loaf.

1 (1/4-oz.) pkg. active dry yeast

1/2 cup warm water (110F, 45C)

3 eggs, lightly beaten

1/2 cup butter, cut into 8 pieces, room temperature

2 tablespoons sugar

1 teaspoon salt

3 to 3-1/2 cups all-purpose flour

1/2 teaspoon coarsely ground black pepper

1/2 teaspoon seasoned pepper

1 egg yolk, lightly beaten

1 teaspoon milk

Seasoned pepper, if desired

In a mixer bowl, sprinkle yeast over water; let stand until softened. Stir in 3 eggs, butter, sugar, salt, yeast mixture and 1 cup flour. Beat 2 minutes. Add peppers. Add enough remaining flour to make a pliable dough. Shape into a ball. Turn out onto a lightly floured surface and knead 7 or 8 minutes until dough is elastic. Grease a bowl; turn dough in bowl to grease all sides. Cover; let rise in a warm draft-free area until doubled in bulk, about 1 hour. Punch down dough; let stand 5 minutes. Grease a 9" x 5" loaf pan. Shape dough and place in pan. Cover with a dry cloth; let rise until doubled in bulk, about 45 minutes. Preheat oven to 375F (190C). In a cup, combine egg yolk and milk; brush on top of loaf. Sprinkle with seasoned pepper, if desired. Bake 40 minutes or until loaf sounds hollow when tapped. If crust becomes too brown, cover with foil last 10 minutes of baking. Cool in pan 5 minutes. Remove from pan; cool. Complete now or make ahead.

To complete now, let stand at room temperature 10 to 15 minutes. Slice and serve warm or at room temperature.

To make ahead, wrap and refrigerate up to 2 days or freeze up to 1 month. Thaw at room temperature. Warm 15 minutes in a 350F (175C) oven, if desired.

1 slice contains:

Cal	Prot	Carb	Fat	Chol	Sodium
216	5g	27g	10g	92mg	259mg

Rhineland Relish *(Cover photo)*

Makes about 2 cups.

1 small green bell pepper, finely chopped

1 small onion, finely chopped

3/4 cup vinegar

1 cup sugar

1/2 teaspoon mustard seeds

1/4 teaspoon celery seeds

2 cups sauerkraut

In a bowl, combine green pepper and onion; set aside. In a saucepan, combine vinegar, sugar, mustard and celery seeds. Bring to a boil. Pour hot syrup over green pepper and onion. Rinse and drain sauerkraut. Add to green-pepper mixture; cover. Complete now or make ahead.

To complete now, refrigerate at least 4 hours. Drain; spoon into a serving dish and serve.

To make ahead, refrigerate up to 24 hours. Drain and serve.

1 tablespoon contains:

Cal	Prot	Carb	Fat	Chol	Sodium
30	0	8g	0	0	98mg

❖ *Incredibly easy to prepare and the perfect accompaniment for your favorite cold cuts.*

Pickled Beets & Cucumbers

Makes 6 servings.

**1 (16-oz.) can sliced
   pickled beets, drained**

**1 cucumber, peeled, thinly
   sliced**

**2 tablespoons minced
   onion**

1 teaspoon sugar

1/4 teaspoon salt

1/8 teaspoon pepper

**1/4 teaspoon dried dill
   weed or 1 teaspoon
   chopped fresh dill**

1/2 cup dairy sour cream

Dill sprig

In a bowl, combine beets, cucumber, onion, sugar, salt, pepper and dill. Stir in sour cream and cover. Complete now or make ahead.

To complete now, refrigerate at least 1 hour. Spoon into a serving bowl; garnish with dill sprig. Serve.

To make ahead, refrigerate up to 24 hours. Serve as directed above.

1 serving contains:

Cal	Prot	Carb	Fat	Chol	Sodium
101	2g	16g	4g	9mg	300mg

Salad Bonanza

❖ *Menu* ❖

Mustard-Sauced Salad
Executive-Suite Platter
Adriatic Summer Salad
Pacific Shrimp Salad
Chinese Chicken Salad
Old-South Loaf
Sourdough Bread
Spiced Island Cookies
Choco-Macadamia Tart, page 125

Serves 10 to 12.

Timetable:

- Spiced Island Cookies – Make and freeze dough up to 1 month. Or refrigerate dough up to 2 weeks.
- Old-South Loaf – Make up to 5 days ahead.
- Pacific Shrimp Salad, Mustard-Sauced Salad and Adriatic Summer Salad – Make up to 24 hours ahead.
- Chinese Chicken Salad – Cook chicken and combine with sauce up to 24 hours ahead. Cook won-ton skins up to 24 hours ahead. Shred lettuce up to 4 hours ahead.
- Choco-Macadamia Tart – Best when made on day it's served; may be made up to 24 hours ahead.

Shortcuts:

- Omit 1 or 2 salads and 1 dessert.
- Buy cooked and shelled seafood.

Mustard-Sauced Salad

2 cups cauliflowerettes, cooked crisp-tender (1/2 medium head)

3 carrots, sliced, cooked crisp-tender

1-1/2 cups sliced mushrooms (1/4 lb.)

2 tablespoons butter or margarine

4 teaspoons all-purpose flour

1/2 cup sugar

1 tablespoon Dijon-style mustard

1/2 cup cider vinegar

1/2 teaspoon salt

1/8 teaspoon pepper

1 small onion, chopped

1 celery stalk, chopped

In a bowl, combine cauliflowerettes, carrots and mushrooms; set aside. In a saucepan, melt butter or margarine; stir in flour. Stirring constantly, cook over medium heat 1 minute. Stir in sugar; then stir in mustard and vinegar. Continue stirring 2 minutes or until translucent and slightly thickened. Remove from heat. Stir in salt, pepper, onion and celery. Pour over vegetables; mix well and cover. Complete now or make ahead.

To complete now, refrigerate at least 2 hours. Drain; spoon into a salad bowl. Serve cold.

To make ahead, refrigerate up to 24 hours. Up to 1 hour before serving, drain.

1 serving contains:

Cal	Prot	Carb	Fat	Chol	Sodium
145	2g	27g	4g	10mg	267mg

Our salad buffet is ideal for a light supper or brunch. Surprise your guests with our version of the Chinese Chicken Salad. Complement salads with a variety of crunchy breads and rolls.

Makes 6 to 8 servings.

Dressing:
1/4 cup olive oil or
  vegetable oil
1/4 cup tarragon vinegar
1/4 cup mayonnaise
1 teaspoon Dijon-style
  mustard
1 tablespoon lemon juice
1/4 teaspoon dried-leaf
  chervil
1/2 teaspoon salt
1/4 teaspoon pepper
2 tablespoons minced
  green onions
1 tablespoon capers,
  drained

1 (14-oz.) can
  artichoke-heart halves
1/2 lb. mushrooms, thinly
  sliced
Boston- or Bibb-lettuce
  leaves
2 tomatoes, cut in wedges
2 ripe avocados, sliced
1/2 lb. shredded cooked
  crabmeat or lobster

To make Dressing, in a blender or food processor fitted with a metal blade, combine oil, vinegar, mayonnaise, mustard, lemon juice, chervil, salt and pepper. Process until blended. Add green onions and capers; briefly process until blended. Pour into a bowl. Drain artichokes; add to dressing. Add mushrooms; toss to coat. Cover. Complete now or make ahead.

To complete now, refrigerate at least 2 hours. Drain, reserving dressing. Arrange lettuce on a serving plate. Spoon drained mushrooms and artichokes onto center of lettuce. Arrange tomato wedges and avocado slices around side. Top with crabmeat or lobster. Spoon reserved dressing over salad or serve dressing separately.

To make ahead, refrigerate up to 24 hours. Remove from refrigerator 20 to 30 minutes before serving. Drain and serve as directed above.

1 serving contains:

Cal	Prot	Carb	Fat	Chol	Sodium
263	9g	13g	22g	27mg	606mg

❖ *Elegant combination of ingredients accented with a blended dressing.*

Adriatic Summer Salad

Makes 6 servings.

4 tomatoes, sliced

1 red onion, thinly sliced

4 oz. mozzarella cheese, thinly sliced

1/2 cup coarsely chopped fresh basil

1/3 cup olive oil

1 tablespoon lemon juice

2 tablespoons red-wine vinegar

1 tablespoon minced parsley

1 garlic clove, crushed

1/4 teaspoon salt

1/4 teaspoon pepper

1/2 teaspoon Dijon-style mustard

1/2 cup sliced pitted ripe olives

Basil sprig

Arrange 1/2 of tomatoes, onion and cheese in a shallow salad bowl. Sprinkle with 1/4 cup chopped basil. Layer remaining tomatoes, onions and cheese. In a bowl, combine oil, lemon juice, vinegar, parsley, garlic, salt, pepper and mustard. Stir until blended. Pour over layered vegetables and cheese. Sprinkle with remaining basil and cover. Complete now or make ahead.

To complete now, refrigerate at least 1 hour. Sprinkle with olive slices; garnish with basil sprig.

To make ahead, refrigerate up to 24 hours. Garnish as directed above.

1 serving contains:

Cal	Prot	Carb	Fat	Chol	Sodium
193	6g	8g	16g	10mg	246mg

Pacific Shrimp Salad

Makes 6 to 8 servings.

**3 cups cold cooked
long-grain white rice**

**1/2 lb. shelled cooked
small shrimp**

**3 oranges or peaches,
peeled, chopped**

**1 cup seedless grapes,
halved**

1/2 cup dairy sour cream

1/2 cup mayonnaise

1 teaspoon curry powder

1/4 teaspoon celery seeds

1/4 teaspoon salt

1/8 teaspoon pepper

2 tablespoons orange juice

1 tablespoon honey

**1/4 cup toasted slivered
almonds**

Lettuce

**1 small cantaloupe or
honeydew melon,
peeled, cut in wedges**

Fluff rice; spoon into a 2-1/2-quart bowl. Top with shrimp, then oranges or peaches and grapes. In a bowl, combine sour cream, mayonnaise, curry powder, celery seeds, salt, pepper, orange juice and honey. Stir until blended; pour over fruit. Sprinkle almonds over top; cover. Complete now or make ahead.

To complete now, refrigerate salad at least 2 hours. Toss to distribute ingredients. Line a salad bowl with lettuce. Spoon salad onto lettuce; garnish with cantaloupe or honeydew melon. Serve immediately.

To make ahead, refrigerate salad up to 24 hours. About 1 hour before serving, toss ingredients. Spoon into lettuce-lined bowl; garnish as directed above. Refrigerate until served.

1 serving contains:

Cal	Prot	Carb	Fat	Chol	Sodium
256	9g	33g	10g	65mg	245mg

❖ *Each bite brings a surprise of different
textures and flavors.*

137

Chinese Chicken Salad

Makes 5 or 6 servings.

4 boneless chicken-breast halves

2 tablespoons vegetable oil

1 tablespoon cornstarch

2 tablespoons soy sauce

1/4 cup hoisin sauce

1 cup chicken broth or bouillon

1/3 cup dry white wine

2 teaspoons sesame oil

1 (8-oz.) can water chestnuts, drained, chopped

1/4 cup chopped green onions

1 tablespoon minced ginger root

6 won-ton skins

1/2 cup vegetable oil

1 small head lettuce

2 tablespoons toasted sesame seeds

Remove skin from chicken; reserve skins. Heat 2 tablespoons oil in a skillet. Add chicken and skins; brown on both sides. Cook 15 minutes or until chicken is done and skins are crisp. Drain on paper towels; reserve drippings in pan. Julienne chicken and skin; set aside. In a cup, stir cornstarch into soy sauce. Add cornstarch mixture, hoisin sauce, broth or bouillon, wine and sesame oil to pan. Stirring, cook over medium heat until translucent. Stir in chicken and skins, water chestnuts, green onions and ginger root; set aside. Stack won-ton skins; cut in quarters. Cut squares in half diagonally. Heat 1/2 cup oil in a skillet. Fry won ton until golden; drain on paper towels. Complete now or make ahead.

To complete now, shred lettuce. In a bowl, combine chicken mixture, shredded lettuce and fried won-ton skins. Sprinkle with sesame seeds. Serve cold.

To make ahead, cover chicken mixture and refrigerate up to 24 hours. Store fried won-ton pieces at room temperature up to 24 hours. About 4 hours before serving, shred lettuce. Serve as directed above.

1 serving contains:

Cal	Prot	Carb	Fat	Chol	Sodium
371	21g	9g	27g	46mg	1089mg

Old-South Loaf

Makes 1 (9" x 5") loaf.

2 cups all-purpose flour

1/2 cup lightly packed brown sugar

1 teaspoon baking powder

1 teaspoon baking soda

1/4 teaspoon ground ginger

1/2 teaspoon ground nutmeg

1/2 teaspoon salt

1/4 cup vegetable oil

3/4 cup milk

2 eggs, lightly beaten

1 cup grated uncooked sweet potato

1 teaspoon grated orange peel

1/2 cup chopped pecans

Grease a 9" x 5" loaf pan; set aside. Preheat oven to 350F (175C). In a bowl, combine flour, brown sugar, baking powder, baking soda, ginger, nutmeg, salt, oil, milk and eggs. Stir until blended. Stir in sweet potato, orange peel and pecans. Spoon into greased pan. Bake 60 to 65 minutes or until a wooden pick inserted in center comes out clean. Remove from pan; cool on a wire rack. Wrap cooled loaf. Complete now or make ahead.

To complete now, refrigerate about 2 hours. Slice and serve.

To make ahead, store up to 24 hours at room temperature or up to 5 days in refrigerator.

1 slice contains:

Cal	Prot	Carb	Fat	Chol	Sodium
214	4g	29g	9g	37mg	208mg

❖ *Discover the subtle flavors in a moist bread that slices beautifully.*

Spiced Island Cookies

Makes 40 to 45 cookies.

1 cup butter or margarine, room temperature

1 cup firmly packed brown sugar

2-1/2 cups all-purpose flour

1/4 teaspoon baking soda

1/2 teaspoon ground nutmeg

2 teaspoons ground cinnamon

1/4 cup dairy sour cream

1/2 cup coarsely chopped cashews

In a bowl, cream butter or margarine and brown sugar until fluffy. In another bowl, blend flour, baking soda, nutmeg and cinnamon. Add dry mixture alternately with sour cream to creamed mixture, beating smooth after each addition. Stir in cashews. Divide dough in half; shape each half into a 2-inch-diameter roll. Complete now or make ahead.

To complete now, wrap in waxed paper; refrigerate 2 hours. Preheat oven to 350F (175C). Cut dough into 1/4-inch slices. Place 2 inches apart on an ungreased baking sheet. Bake 10 minutes. Remove and cool on a rack. Serve.

To make ahead, wrap dough rolls in waxed paper and place in freezer bags. Freeze up to 1 month. Or refrigerate dough up to 2 weeks. Thaw frozen dough in refrigerator. Cut, bake and serve as directed above.

1 cookie contains:

Cal	Prot	Carb	Fat	Chol	Sodium
92	1g	11g	5g	12mg	42mg

❖ *There is always room for a simple accompaniment to after-dinner coffee or tea.*

Ice-Cream Social

❖ *Menu* ❖

Lemon-Ginger Sorbet
Vanilla Ice Cream
White-Chocolate Ice Cream
Licorice-Chip Ice Cream
Melba Sauce
Peanut-Fudge Sauce
Orange-Pecan Topping
Tropics Fruit & Nut Mix
Spiced Island Cookies, page 140

Serves 20.

Timetable:

- Spiced Island Cookies – Make and freeze dough up to 1 month. Or refrigerate dough up to 2 weeks.
- Peanut-Fudge Sauce – Make up to 1 month ahead.
- Tropics Fruit & Nut Mix and Orange-Pecan Topping – Make up to 3 weeks ahead.
- If using your own ice cubes, start making and storing about 7 days ahead.
- Frozen Desserts – Four days before, begin making 1 or 2 desserts each day.
- Melba Sauce – Make up to 3 days ahead.
- Up to 24 hours ahead, assemble dishes and utensils.

Shortcuts:

- Except for specific flavors and dry toppings, purchase all or any part of the menu.
- Create your own toppings.

Lemon-Ginger Sorbet

Makes about 1 quart.

2-1/2 cups water

1 cup sugar

1-1/2 teaspoons grated ginger root

2/3 cup lemon juice

1 teaspoon grated lemon peel

In a saucepan, combine water and sugar. Stir constantly over low heat until sugar dissolves. Stir in ginger root, lemon juice and lemon peel; cool to room temperature. Pour into ice-cream canister. Freeze according to manufacturer's directions. Complete now or make ahead.

To complete now, store in freezer 1 to 3 hours until firm. Serve at once.

To make ahead, store in freezer up to 4 days.

1 serving contains:

Cal	Prot	Carb	Fat	Chol	Sodium
101	0	27g	0	0	1mg

Have an old-fashioned ice-cream social. Serve a variety of frozen desserts and tasty sauces. Guests add toppings, chopped cookies, crushed candies or crunchy granola and nuts for extra flavor.

Vanilla Ice Cream

Makes about 2 quarts.

1-1/3 cups sugar

1 tablespoon cornstarch

1/4 teaspoon salt

3 cups whole milk

2 egg yolks

1 (5.33-oz.) can evaporated milk

1 cup whipping cream

1 tablespoon vanilla extract

In a saucepan, combine sugar, cornstarch and salt. Stir in whole milk. Stir over medium heat until mixture begins to simmer. Simmer 1 minute over low heat. In a bowl, lightly beat egg yolks. Stir about 1 cup milk mixture into egg yolks; stir egg-yolk mixture into remaining milk mixture. Stirring constantly, cook over low heat 2 minutes or until slightly thickened. Stir in evaporated milk, cream and vanilla. Cool to room temperature. Pour into ice-cream canister. Freeze according to manufacturer's directions. Complete now or make ahead.

To complete now, store in freezer 1 to 3 hours until firm. Serve at once.

To make ahead, store in freezer up to 4 days.

1 serving contains:

Cal	Prot	Carb	Fat	Chol	Sodium
165	3g	20g	8g	56mg	73mg

Variation: Chocolate Ice Cream – Substitute 2 whole eggs for egg yolks. Reduce vanilla extract to 1 teaspoon. Stir 3 ounces melted semi-sweet chocolate into warm egg-milk mixture. Complete as directed above.

143

Makes about 2 quarts.

1/2 lb. white chocolate
2 tablespoons butter
1 cup milk
5 egg yolks
1/4 cup sugar
1 tablespoon light corn
    syrup
2 cups whipping cream

Cut chocolate into small pieces. In a 2-quart saucepan, combine chocolate, butter and milk. Stir constantly over very low heat until chocolate and butter melt; remove from heat. In a mixer bowl, beat egg yolks and sugar about 5 minutes. Stir egg-yolk mixture and corn syrup into chocolate mixture. Stirring constantly, cook over low heat 8 to 10 minutes until thickened and mixture coats a metal spoon. Remove from heat; stir in cream. Cool to room temperature. Pour into ice-cream canister. Freeze according to manufacturer's directions. Complete now or make ahead.

To complete now, store in freezer 1 to 3 hours until firm. Serve at once.

To make ahead, store in freezer up to 4 days.

1 serving contains:

Cal	Prot	Carb	Fat	Chol	Sodium
237	3g	14g	19g	113mg	49mg

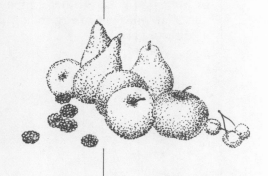

Licorice-Chip Ice Cream

Makes about 2 quarts.

**6 to 8 oz. hollow
  licorice-candy twists**
3/4 cup sugar
1 tablespoon cornstarch
1/4 teaspoon salt
2 cups milk
2 cups half and half
2 egg yolks
1 cup whipping cream
1 teaspoon anise extract

Place licorice in freezer 2 hours before making ice cream. In a saucepan, combine sugar, cornstarch and salt; stir in milk and 1 cup half and half. Stirring constantly, cook over low heat about 5 minutes or until slightly thickened; remove from heat. In a bowl, beat egg yolks. Gradually stir about 1 cup milk mixture into beaten egg yolks. Stir egg-yolk mixture into remaining milk mixture. Stirring constantly, cook over low heat 8 to 10 minutes until thickened and mixture coats a metal spoon. Remove from heat; cool to room temperature. Add remaining half and half, whipping cream and anise extract. Place licorice in a heavy plastic bag. Crush with a mallet. Do not add licorice to cream mixture until ready to freeze ice cream. Licorice dissolves in unfrozen cream mixture. Add crushed licorice to cream mixture. Pour into ice-cream canister. Immediately freeze according to manufacturer's directions. Complete now or make ahead.

To complete now, store in freezer 1 to 3 hours until firm. Serve at once.

To make ahead, store in freezer up to 4 days.

1 serving contains:

Cal	Prot	Carb	Fat	Chol	Sodium
187	3g	22g	10g	61mg	71mg

❖ *Young and old alike enjoy this unusual combination.*

Melba Sauce

Makes about 1-1/2 cups.

**1 (12-oz.) pkg. frozen
 unsweetened red
 raspberries or 3 cups
 fresh red raspberries**
1/2 cup sugar
2 teaspoons cornstarch

Thaw berries if frozen. In blender or food
processor fitted with a metal blade, purée
berries. Strain purée through 2 thicknesses of
damp cheesecloth or a fine sieve to remove
seeds; discard seeds. In a 1-quart saucepan,
combine sugar and cornstarch; stir in purée.
Stirring constantly, cook over low heat 4 to 5
minutes until slightly thickened. Cover and cool
to room temperature. Complete now or make
ahead.

To complete now, refrigerate 2 hours or until
thoroughly chilled.

To make ahead, refrigerate covered up to
3 days.

1 tablespoon contains:

Cal	Prot	Carb	Fat	Chol	Sodium
24	0	6g	0	0	0

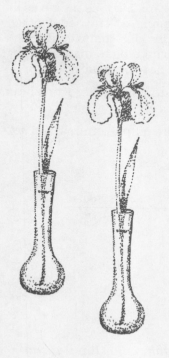

❖ *A lovely sauce to crown your ice cream, cake
    or pancakes.*

Peanut-Fudge Sauce

Makes about 2 cups

1-1/2 cups sugar

1/4 teaspoon salt

1 cup milk or half and half

1 tablespoon butter or margarine

3 oz. semi-sweet chocolate, chopped

1/2 cup chunk-style peanut butter

1/2 teaspoon vanilla extract

In a saucepan, combine sugar, salt and milk or half and half; stir until blended. Add butter or margarine and chocolate. Cook over low heat, stirring occasionally, until sugar dissolves and butter and chocolate melt. Simmer 5 to 6 minutes. Stir in peanut butter until blended. Remove from heat; stir in vanilla. Complete now or make ahead.

To complete now, cover and cool to room temperature.

To make ahead, cover and refrigerate up to 1 month. Bring to room temperature before serving.

1 tablespoon contains:

Cal	Prot	Carb	Fat	Chol	Sodium
80	1g	12g	4g	2mg	43mg

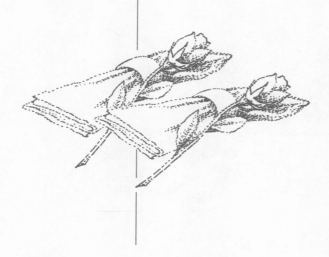

Orange-Pecan Topping

Makes 1-1/2 cups.

5 tablespoons brown sugar

1/2 teaspoon ground cinnamon

1/4 teaspoon ground nutmeg

1-1/2 cups pecan pieces or halves

1/3 cup orange juice

Preheat oven to 350F (175C). In a bowl, combine 2 tablespoons brown sugar, 1/4 teaspoon cinnamon and 1/8 teaspoon nutmeg. Spread over bottom of an ungreased 9-inch-square baking pan. In same bowl, combine remaining brown sugar, cinnamon and nutmeg; set aside. In another bowl, combine pecans and orange juice. Stir until all nuts are wet. Pour nuts into a sieve and drain. Spread nuts over mixture in pan. Sprinkle with reserved brown sugar. Bake 25 minutes, stirring at least twice. Spread on foil to cool. Complete now or make ahead.

To complete now, serve when cooled.

To make ahead, store covered at room temperature up to 3 weeks.

1 tablespoon contains:

Cal	Prot	Carb	Fat	Chol	Sodium
61	1g	5g	5g	0	1mg

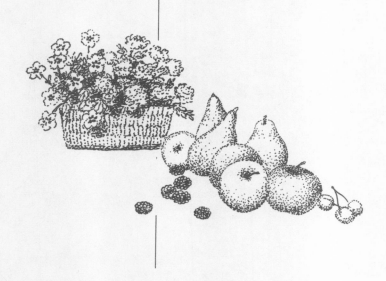

Tropics Fruit & Nut Mix

Makes about 1-1/2 cups.

5 tablespoons sugar
1 teaspoon ground ginger
1/3 cup slivered almonds
1/3 cup shaved coconut
1/3 cup raisins
**1/3 cup chopped dried
  papaya or dried apricots**
1/3 cup pineapple juice

Spread 2 tablespoons sugar over bottom of a 9-inch-square baking pan. Sprinkle 1/2 teaspoon ginger over top. Preheat oven to 350F (175C). In a bowl, combine almonds, coconut, raisins, papaya or apricots and pineapple juice; stir well. Strain fruit to remove excess pineapple juice. Spread mixture over sugar in pan. Top with remaining 3 tablespoons sugar and 1/2 teaspoon ginger. Bake 25 minutes or until almonds begin to brown, stirring at least twice. Spread on foil to cool; separate clusters. Complete now or make ahead.

To complete now, serve when cooled.

To make ahead, store covered at room temperature up to 3 weeks.

1 tablespoon contains:

Cal	Prot	Carb	Fat	Chol	Sodium
34	0	6g	1g	0	1mg

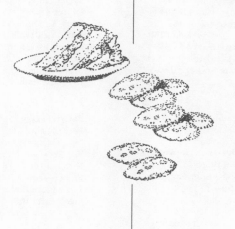

Index